THE WIDOW OF VRINDAVAN

THE WIDOW OF VRINDAVAN

Kusum Ansal

Vitasta
Let Knowledge Spread

Published by
Renu Kaul Verma
Vitasta Publishing Pvt Ltd
2/15, Ansari Road, Daryaganj
New Delhi - 110 002
info@vitastapublishing.com

ISBN 9789386473042

First Edition 2017

Second Reprint 2021

MRP ₹350

Disclaimer
All persons portrayed in this book are fictitious. Any resemblance to real persons, living or dead, is purely co-incidental.Though this is a work of fiction, opinions expressed in it are the author's own. The publisher is in no way responsible for these.

Cover and layout by Vits Press
Printed by Thomson Press (India) Ltd.

Author's Note

I HAVE GROWN and lived in an Aryasamaji atmosphere with faith in a formless and universal God. My creed had protected me from superstitious beliefs. At a subconscious level, however, I have always had the desire to enquire into things through research and experiment. I walked through the streets of Vrindavan and did darshan at temples in pursuit of this belief. More than the spirituality and sanctity of this sacred city,what left its impress upon me was the greed of the pandits, the commercialization of religion, and its brutal exploitation of the vulnerable and weak.

In an Indian context, to get married and widowed is the easiest way to exploitation. Treading mechanically down the pathways of Vrindavan, I often found myself among destitute, skeletal widows whose presence was profoundly disturbing to me. I gazed with willing tears at these weary and sad-eyed travellers. They stirred me. They challenged me. They put me in a dilemma as to how to react to them. What to do about them? Many and varied were my experiences, thoughts and emotions, but all I could do was to reveal to society the painful reality of these homelss widows—especially the ones who had come, or had been chased away from Bengal, to live in grotty ashrams where they were mistreated, tortured, starved and sold. Doing twelve-hour jaaps, subsisting on two rotis a day, shaven, shorn, abused and made sub-human—the bleak and relentless exploitation of these widows, in the name of religion, is a travesty of our faith.

Part I

SHE WOKE UP feeling dizzy. Waves of intense pain coursed through her body. Her wide-open, bloodshot eyes held a deep, stony stillness and the swell of unshed tears and horrible images oppressed her body. She rose slowly from the ground, trying desperately to cover herself with her tattered clothing. Staving off the waves of giddiness, she tried to figure out where she was. The room in which she found herself was dark and discoloured with smoke-stained walls and no windows, so there was no question of fresh air. There was just one door with a rusted hinge, its cracked shutter dangling. She was not sure whether it was open or shut. Trying to dispel the blankness from her mind she began the process of returning to herself. Still she could muster no immediate recollection of where she was. She dimly recalled a two day train journey with no idea of where it had brought her. What place is this? What city?

And why am I here? Not one letter or name lent itself to her mind. She looked around and noticed a few bundled up shapes lying this way and that on the floor beside her. Who were these people? Sleeping right next to her was the tallish, dark woman of the night before; beside her was another, her body trembling from head to toe. Who are these women? How am I connected to them? She rummaged through the pitiful bundle with her which contained the four saris she possessed. But it wasn't a sari she was looking for. She was rummaging through the bundle for the blue notebook in which she used to write now and then. The blue notebook, which was a chronicle of her experiences.

A wave of dizziness came over her again and she felt faint. Raising herself unsteadily from the floor, she leaned against the wall for a moment and then staggered to the door pushing it open and stepping outside. The fresh air revived her. She found herself in a long corridor that led to a courtyard with a water tap in one corner. The courtyard was littered with trash. The piles of garbage on the broken floor seemed to mock her. The corridor was empty but soon a woman emerged from nowhere, out of some mysterious corner, and going straight to the tap began to bathe under it. She straightened on seeing Tapasi.

'Oho! It is you—the new arrival! You haven't been spared by her, I can see.' The woman snickered baring dirty teeth. Tapasi wondered how to respond to the woman. She felt as if she had just woken from a long, drugged sleep, as if she had been jolted awake from a relentless nightmare. And her body? Her body felt like a stick of sugarcane from which the last drops of juice had been squeezed.

She looked around and watched a clear blue dawn break over the tiled roof of the ramshackle building. She had not seen the morning in a long time. The sight of the sun peering from behind a tree energized her. There were other women at the tap now. They made room for her. 'Come, take a bath,' one of them said encouragingly. Wrapping her torn sari closer, Tapasi walked up to the water tap and doused her face. As her vision cleared she noticed that clumps of hair had been yanked out of her head, her arms were bruised blue and there were teeth marks, lesions and scratches all over her body. Are these people cannibals? What place is this? What am I doing here?

Tapasi sat under the flowing tap. She did not care if the water was hot or cold, or what season it was. Wasn't it enough that her body was getting cleansed? There is something about water that not only cleanses the body but revitalizes it too.

The first bather returned dressed in a white sari bordered with black. 'Enough bathing now,' she said. 'You have used up too much water, the others have to bathe too.'

'Yes, of course.' Tapasi left the tap and started to take out a not too clean sari from her bundle when the woman handed her a coarse white sari with a black border, similar to the one she was wearing. 'Here, wear this.'

Pushing her wet hair off her forehead, Tapasi wiped her tresses with the torn sari she had taken off. Then, not knowing where to go, she crossed the veranda and entered a room. It was cold. Stale, musty air pervaded it. A low-powered bulb gave off a faint, dim light that seemed to mock the gloom. A few women stood around chatting among themselves. The black-skinned woman from the night before, the one who had lain next to her, stood facing them. She was talking loudly and her abrasive words were like hot, molten glass poured into Tapasi's ears. Her conduct of the night before flashed through Tapasi's mind. She took in the shaven heads and terrified faces of the other women and wondered if she was in hell. Are these people humans, cannibals, demons or some other species? Each pore of Tapasi's body exhorted her to retreat and run home. What will become of me here? Is being a widow and being banished from my world not bad enough? Surely the thinking in my hometown is not that backward, surely my people don't have *such* stunted minds. But then why am I here? Tapasi touched a hand to her damp hair. Surrounded by so many women with shaven heads, her long hair made her stand out. Quickly she pulled her sari pallu over her head.

The women had lined up now and one of them was handing out glasses of tea. Tapasi too was handed a stainless steel tumbler of hot tea. She could not remember when she had had her last meal and gulped down the tea quickly. The women began to sing a bhajan.

'Mere to giridhar gopal doosra na koi.'

(Girdhar Gopal is my only true love)

The words of the song transported Tapasi to the Magh Mela of Bolepur. To the morning session of the music concert. And Jatin Da.

'Jaa ke sir mormukut mero pati soi.'

(The one who wears a peacock plume coronet is my husband).

Husband? thought Tapasi. What is this thing called 'husband'? What a filthy trick it had been. That man who called himself my 'husband', barged into my life when I'd been happily engrossed in school, with only a burning desire to learn more and make something of my life.

Her reverie was broken by a middle-aged woman who poked her with a stick. 'Hey stand straight!' she admonished. Then she opened a register of sorts and barked, 'What is your name?'

'Taposhi.'

'Say "Tapasi" not "Taposhi". I don't know why you Bengali dames roll each word around in your mouths. Are you a widow, Tapasi?'

'Yes.' Tapasi wondered if she was a policewoman. She had never seen a policewoman before.

She entered her name in the register. Village—Bolepur,

West Bengal. Husband's name? What was his name? Oh, yes—Naren Majumdar. He'd died some time ago. How could he have lived anyway, in such poor health and with such an acute shortness of breath? She'd been a widow for a while now. She'd been married to him for a year, maybe two. Vermilion in the parting of her hair, a shell bangle on her arm, a coloured sari. That is all he'd given her though he'd given a lot more to Kaka in exchange for her. And what had she given him? Her body, her studies, her future and her dreams.

'If you are a widow then how come they have not tonsured your hair yet? Come on, move forward. You better learn the rules and regulations of this place, you hear me?'

The bhajan ended. The women were each handed two rotis and a muddy looking cooked vegetable wrapped in paper. Hunger knows no discrimination. Tapasi's fingers were accustomed to handling rice and she found it difficult to tackle the rotis, yet her appetite was stimulated. She could not remember when she had eaten last.

'May I have some more?' Tapasi put out her hand.

The collective whoop of laughter startled her. They were all looking at her. The baton-wielding senior glared at them. 'Silence!' she shouted. Then turning to Tapasi, she said, 'You silly fool! This is all the food you'll get each day. Move on, everybody. Time to go to the temple. Whose turn is it today?'

As the women began to file out of the room, one of

them quietly placed half a roti on Tapasi's upturned palm and said gently, 'Here, eat it. And come with me. I'll explain everything to you.'

Tapasi shoved the roti into her mouth and wolfed it down. She had a drink of water from the tap and began to follow the others not knowing where she was going. As if only her shadow self, and not she, were moving. So where am I? Who am I? Taposhi? Or Tapasi?

Stepping out of the building, Tapasi read the board on the outer gate. 'Sri Radha Krishna Vidhwa Ashram'. Radha and Krishna were lovers. An ashram for widows named after the divine lovers? Wasn't that incongruous? Jatin Da used to say, 'You ask too many questions. Your name should have been Prashna instead of Taposhi...Prashna, The one who asks Questions!'

◆◆◆

Picking her way through a stinking narrow alley, she finally asked, 'What place is this?'

'It is Vrindavan. Don't you know?' The woman walking beside her said.

'Why am I here?'

'It is the abode of God. Widows who reside here attain Paradise. Those who live here are absolved of the sins of all their past and future births.'

Tapasi looked at the filth all around and read the signboards on the streets and crossings. 'Radha Krishna

Chowk', 'Gokul Dham', 'Raghav Halwai', 'Badri Gaushala'. Guru Dada had told her that Paradise was the place where God resided. Could this be that place?

They stopped—the whole jingbang. The doors of the temple in front of them opened. Now they were all kneeling to touch their foreheads to the threshold of the temple which had been blunted by the touch and friction of countless heads over the decades. Now they were entering the temple. A chessboard courtyard stretched out before them. Tapasi felt giddy and the black and white tiles merged with each other.

They entered a large room where other women, dressed like them in white saris, were straightening up from the threadbare dhurries on the floor. The newcomers took their place. Tapasi was astonished by the exquisite beauty of the idols. Yes, I recognize them. Lord Krishna and Radhika. The idols were breathtaking. They're the same as the Gods in the picture calendar in Dada's house! A winsome couple with smiling faces, their figures inclining towards each other; a captivating attitude, an unsurpassable charm.

Dressed in yellow kurtas and white dhotis, a couple of pandits with tilaks of sandalwood paste and roli on their foreheads and a long tuft of hair dangling from their otherwise tonsured heads, bustled about the temple. They anointed the idols with milk, curd, honey, ghee, water and sandalwood paste amidst the chanting of mantras. Then they bathed the idols with water from a huge vessel. After wiping the idols dry with a clean towel, the priests began to dress them. Decked in silver and gold jewellery and adorned with flowers, the enchanting idols seemed to smile serenely at the devotees. It was Tapasi's first exposure to so much beauty, to dresses and jewellery as splendid as these. She was captivated. She was reminded of the temple of Ma Kali at Bolepur where she had never quite got a proper look at the idol of the Goddess because of its dazzling brilliance—indeed, it had been quite impossible for a frail girl like her to gaze intently at Ma Kali's idol. Of course she had worshipped idols of the Goddess, but those had been ones which had been created only to be immersed during the puja festival. Never had she seen such beauty nor been as enchanted as she was now.

Besides, Rakhal Kaka had had no truck with God. His entire existence revolved around a meal of jhol, bhat and salt followed by work—a tired body drenched in perspiration, and then drowned in toddy. She'd grown up unmindful of His presence, going about her household chores, attending school and curling up to sleep in a corner of the house at night. Her only exposure to God and the universe He'd created was through her books or the morning prayer, the *Vaitalik*, at school.

Other than this, she learnt about God through her

conversations with Jatin Da and Kanika Didi. Jatin Da often said, *'Manusher monchay manusheri mon.'* (The human heart longs for human intimacy).

'And how about God?' She would ask.

'God is a presence in whom we have faith. We don't position our faith in the material world because it is tangible as well as changeable. But God is permanent. We all, including you Taposhi, are Hindus. All you should do is to have faith in God. Try to know him. God is wisdom to us.'

Kanika Didi would laugh at such conversations. She would say, 'You make such sage utterances in front of a young girl like her! She is like an uncut rock that needs to be chiselled and polished.'

And now, sitting there in that temple it was as if the rock was melting by degrees. She remembered reading, 'The earth, the sky and man are all contained in God.' In which case the idols too were deities incarnate. Time past began to dissolve into time present. A wondrous entirely new feeling stirred her heart.

The spell was broken when the woman sitting next to her handed her a tiny pair of cymbals tied together with a piece of string. Flustered, Tapasi said, 'But I don't know how to play them!' Her shrill protest echoed through the silence of the temple. People turned and stared at her. The black-skinned woman muttered something and scowled darkly. Terrified, Tapasi lost her voice and sat with her eyes closed. Then the musical instruments came alive and enveloped in the fragrance of burning incense the melodious chanting of mantras commenced. Tapasi tentatively struck the cymbals together.

Sri Radhey Gobinda man bhajle, Sri Radhey Gobinda.

The cymbals in her hand settled into the beat. A slight tremor played on her lips. The sequence of bhajans continued unbroken. Tapasi lost herself in the music. She had a sense of something melting and evaporating within her. Oblivion gave her a feeling of even greater hollowness than the one she was accustomed to, as if she was not a body but an earthen pitcher, empty of all water. She lost all sense of time.

The women were getting up from their places. Still lightheaded, Tapasi had barely stood up when a woman snatched the cymbals from her hands and sat down in the place vacated by her. Her group came out of the temple just as another waiting outside began to enter the hall. Tapasi was tired. Her compatriots looked exhausted, almost half dead. She turned to look back and saw that the other party had already commenced their jaap of *Sri Radhey Gobinda*. She thought that the idol of Radha, sitting calmly earlier, was now smiling softly. The pearl drop in her nose ring seemed to sway gently. Why does God want to listen to His name being chanted all the time and that too from the tongues of these pathetic, crushed, broken and banished widows?

Questions again, she thought, but more than questions, her body was in the grip of exhaustion. She was about to pass out when two women steadied her and helped her sit on the floor. She felt light. Can people hold up a shadow? When she opened her eyes, she saw the black-skinned woman sprinkling water on her face. She held the lota to her mouth and Tapasi drank thirstily from it.

'What is your name? You are so weak. You faint again and again.'

'What is in a name?' ventured Tapasi.

'Tell me now or I'll ask you at night.' The woman laughed crudely.

The night—that frightful night—flashed in front of Tapasi's eyes. The long journey, over two days and nights, at the end of which a retainer of the Majumdar clan had pushed her through the door of the ashram and disappeared, had left her feeling hollow. She'd been hungry and thirsty and thoroughly fatigued. Unable to make sense of the recent upheavals in her life she had sat down helplessly. At length she'd stretched on the floor and, resting her head on the small bundle she was carrying, had fallen into a troubled sleep, only to be woken with a start, to the prickly feel of a pair of hands groping and fondling her. In the half darkness of the room she had seen a black woman bending over her. Her sari had been pushed up round her thighs and the woman was stretched over her like an evil spirit. Tapasi had shouted and screamed but the other women in the room had watched impassively. The teeth of the aggressor, accompanied by stinking saliva drooling from her mouth, bruised and stamped Tapasi's body. It was difficult to believe that one woman could send another into such a state of physical resistance and protest that the latter lost consciousness.

Dark shadows of fear began to surround Tapasi once again. She felt a sinking sensation. As if she was drowning within herself. When she'd been on the train, a couple of women had told her that God resided in Kashi and Vrindavan. They'd said that these were holy places where widows found peace—where sins were washed away. Where they would attain salvation. That was why she was being sent to Vrindavan to pray and worship. So this is the seat of God? How much more tyranny must I endure and for how long? She did not know.

Tapasi tried to move away from the crowd of women when someone placed an orange in her hands. She looked around and noticed that the women were again sitting in an attitude of supplication. A fat woman, dripping with jewellery and affluence, a heavy silver keyring dangling at her ample waist, was distributing prasad. Tapasi's being was in total contrast to hers. A frail figure draped in a black bordered white sari. A shadow within a shadow. What direction has my life taken? Who was I once and who am I now? Widow, beggar, woman, hunger—How come these are the only words that come to my mind?

Immediately hunger became the dominant image in her consciousness. Tapasi began to eat the orange hurriedly for fear it may be snatched away by someone else. All the women were gobbling their oranges in the same way. Is hunger such an abject state?

Thinking again of the dark-skinned woman, Tapasi realized that it was not courage but timidity that had helped her pull her hand away from her grip and walk at a distance from her. A feeling of rebellion rose within her. I will not identify myself with this rag-tag band of beggar women. Their faces reminded her of the hungry and thirsty children with shrivelled up black bodies that she had seen in a documentary at school. Their skin had clung so tightly to their emaciated little bodies that she could count their ribs. Their unblinking eyes, as hundreds of flies flitted around their faces, were full of petrified pain. She could never forget that scene. The children were so weak they could not even lift their hands to wave off the flies. What was their country called? Somalia. And those women with their dried out breasts. Weeping women who could not carry out the responsibilities of motherhood. What is Somalia like? Where is it? Why has God marked out women and children for so much suffering? Or was Somalia just a case in point, to create terror, a fearful spectacle, forming and fading out by turn in ones mind? What was the reality behind it? Jatin

Da had not been home the day she had seen the Somalian children so she had not been able to ask him. Why do so many questions trouble my mind? Why is the search for answers at once hidden and revealed?

◆◆◆

Returning to the ashram the women busied themselves. The stick-wielding woman of the morning was talking to some people in the office. The women in charge of the food were chopping onions and potatoes. Tapasi was handed a broom. The place was really dirty. As she moved along on her haunches, sweeping the trash and dust out of her path, she found a woman writhing in pain in a room at the far end of the ashram. Even though the woman was groaning in agony she was trying to pat and soothe a little girl who sat crying by her side. The child was not more than three or four years old. Tapasi noticed the tears of the suffering woman but went about quietly sweeping the floor. She realized that the ragged blanket with which the woman was covered was entirely inadequate. As she drew closer to where the woman lay, the woman asked in a voice quivering in pain, 'Could you get me some water?'

Tapasi picked up a dirty little plastic mug lying near the woman. She rinsed it out, then filled it with water from the tap and brought it back.

'Are you in a lot of pain? Shall I massage your head?' Tapasi sat down beside the woman.

'No,' she answered. She was holding her stomach. A spasm rocked her body.

'Have you taken some medicine?'

'Medicine?' Another spasm went through her.

'Hey you...why are you sitting around leaving all the filth about? Get up, finish your work and go to the office after that, Behenji is calling you,' a woman shouted menacingly at her.

Tapasi got up, collected the trash in a crumpled plastic bag and dumped it in a large drum placed at the entrance of the ashram. In the process, she also tried to familiarize herself with her surroundings. The rough, unpaved backyard stank of the garbage strewn everywhere. A few skeletal trees stood forlorn, with no leaves on their branches, adding to the desolation of the place.

Tapasi went to the office and stood with her head bowed in front of Behenji. There was a huge pile of brand new blankets in the room. The rich woman who'd handed out the oranges in the temple was sitting in a chair and talking to the cane-wielding woman.

'Ambikaji, please distribute these blankets amongst the widows. There are sixty of them. It is Sethji's sixtieth birthday today. Could you please give them away on my behalf? I am in a hurry, otherwise I would personally have handed them over to every inmate.' The rich woman stood up.

'Don't worry, Sethaniji. This ashram functions on the

bounty of philanthropists like you. These widows have nothing when they come here. Through the generous donations of people like you, they take back boxes full of treasure to their homes...'

'You are so dedicated. One should learn the art of service from you.'

'Thank you so much. I heard Sethji is granting an award for social service this year. Tell him not to forget me...'

'Of course. Who could be more deserving than you?'

They both beamed at each other and moved towards the door.

Ambika Devi came back to her office after seeing off the rich woman and sprawled out inelegantly on the divan. She noticed Tapasi waiting in a corner of the room. 'Oh, it is you! Here, take this key, open the store and put these blankets in there. Lock the door after you are done.'

Tapasi unlocked the door and started picking up the blankets. When she carried them in, she noticed that the store was crammed with stuff—clothes, utensils, food packets and a whole lot of other goods.

'Could I give a blanket to the sick woman down there, with your permission? Her blanket is in tatters.'

'Oh my! Such concern! You've hardly been here a day and you dare to speak out so much! Why should I give her a blanket? Has it come free? Lord knows where you come from—all you bloodsuckers! Listen you chit of a girl...

what is your name? Whatever your name may be...there are certain rules and regulations of the ashram which the inmates have to observe carefully. Only the ones who serve at the temple reside here. You have to go for jaap—for six hours. All you get is two dhotis and two rotis. Nothing more! Do you understand? And mind you, keep your eyes ahead of you and don't talk to anyone on your way to and from the temple. Duties are shared in the ashram. Each person has to work according to a schedule. A week of cleaning the ashram, a week of washing utensils, followed by a week of cooking, understand? And yes, don't ever try to sneak out of this place! That close relative of yours, the one who dropped you here, will be in touch with me about you! You are in my charge from now on.'

Tapasi came out of the office. The corridor was redolent with the appetizing smell of fresh rotis being cooked but the food made at that hour was intended for those who did the jaap in the evening. Each inmate was entitled to just two rotis and she had already eaten her share.

The groans of the sick woman now reached the corridor. Tapasi went to the water tap and drank some water. Then she returned to the room and lay down on a torn dhurrie spread close to the wall. The room was so dimly lit that there was nothing else one could do there and the fatigue of her frail body soon translated into an exhausted sleep.

But at an unknown hour in the night she woke up

with a start and found someone mounting her. Instantly, Tapasi knew that it was the same repugnant, black woman pounding and mauling her, pulling at her flesh like wet clay. She knew what she was in for. She had been as brutally tormented by her sickly husband who, struggling with his own inadequacies and disease, gasping for breath, would kiss and lick her body, grab and pinch and scratch her all over. Then, just as she was beginning to get aroused, he would turn over and fall asleep, leaving her alone to drift in the desolation of a body in which strange new desires rose only to crash into a brambly bush and then stalk off, leaving her body sore. She had lived through three or four years of scratches, grappling, beating and pain. Until Majumdar Moshai left for his heavenly abode and her husband's relatives summarily took possession of the house where she'd spent her thorny marital life under the illusion that it was her home. Stripped of everything and dumped here—in a home for widows in Vrindavan, the sacred city, a step away from salvation. But what did she get? Black Barota's savage lust. Suddenly, she felt a surge of determination rush through her body. Whatever her external self had suffered, her inner self, her self-esteem was poised exactly where it had stood on the last day of her final school leaving examination.

Tapasi pushed Barota away, and sat up screaming with all her might. Shoving violently, she threw her off her body.

'I'll smash your arm if you touch me again. Understand?' Tapasi shouted. There was fire in her eyes.

'You'll smash my arm? You? You should know that I have come here after slicing off the hands of my husband with a scythe! Do you have the guts to touch my arm? Who do you think you are? None of these women dare defy me.' Barota shouted back as loudly.

Tapasi warded off Barota's outstretched arms and screamed again. It was an extraordinary scream. Not only Barota, all the others present were struck by its poignant intensity. A woman who screamed like that deserved extra attention. Even Barota, heartless tyrant that she was, stopped in her tracks listening to that scream, struck suddenly by the idea that similar tormented screams were emanating from the beings of all the other women present in the room. She was nonplussed. It was the first time that her aggressive, fearless self was touched by a feeling like fear. Chastened and subdued, she let go of Tapasi's trembling hands and slunk away to the part of the room where her bedding was spread.

Later in the night, glancing at Barota's sleeping figure, Tapasi thought how much like a boa constrictor she looked —twisted, black and coiled up. God knew when she would strike again, and squeeze an unsuspecting victim to death.

Silently, they all noted that Barota was the only one to get a new blanket and that her sheets were spotlessly clean. Tapasi wrapped the sari that she had brought with her from home around her body to protect herself from the cold. The darkness of the night and the chill stretched endlessly. The darkness was a symbol of her denial, it was the truth stretched between her self and reality—a reality that was getting bleaker by degrees and which she was being forced to accept.

◆◆◆

Over the days, Tapasi came to learn a little more about the lives of the other women who shared her cell with her. Noorabai, was the widow of Tulsi Ahir from Barpani Pada in Orissa. Village Bolegir had been hit by drought and Tulsi Ahir had nothing to fall back upon—neither land nor property. He was a daily wage agricultural worker with a wife and four children to support. To make matters worse, Tulsi had a paralytic attack and was severely disabled. There was absolutely no food in the house. Around the same time, the practice of pledging children for money had gained popularity. Taking her eight-year-old daughter, Sanju, by the hand, Noora visited the moneylender of Mundapur. Sanju was pledged away for two kilos of millet and a hundred and fifty rupees. It had been the easiest way out for the family's survival. Soon three-year-old Mithu and eighteen-month-old Nanda were 'given away for adoption'. Ironically, the ones for whose sake the children were pledged away, succumbed to hunger and drought. Noora was the only one to survive and she, exploited and pushed around, had somehow found her way to the ashram. The jaap at the temple, and the promise of salvation on two rotis and two dhotis—that is what she had ended up with. Noorabai used to weep alone in a dark corner of the ashram every night. Hunger was the greatest reality of her life, a reality more sticky than the feel of her bitter tears.

Noorabai did not even know what her religion was—whether she was Hindu or Muslim. Married off in her early teens she had had four children in quick succession and then her husband had fallen ill. Drought, separation from her children and widowhood—struggling against such odds, where is the scope for God and religion? Hunger, grief and the desolation of being abandoned, were the realities of her life. When Tapasi asked her why she cried so much, Noorabai replied, 'Because I am shattered. I find some relief in tears. What else can I do?'

Tapasi grew thoughtful at Noora's answer. She felt no sorrow about leaving Kaka's home, the death of Majumdar Babu or her state of widowhood. Her eyes were devoid of tears though she was restless with unfulfilled desires and unrealized aspirations. There was resentment at the sudden suspension of her education and the shattering of her dreams. It had led to a kind of anger but against whom? Kaka, Jatin Da, Kanika Di—there was no one whom she could really call her own.

Tapasi would notice Vrinda groaning with pain everyday and feel sorry for her. However, even in the middle of all her torment, Vrinda took care to massage the crooked legs of her little daughter. Tapasi was deeply moved by this.

'Is that what the meaning of the word suffering is?' Tapasi would ask.

'Maybe,' the equally naive Vrinda answered, nodding her head as she explained to Tapasi, 'I am only familiar with pain. I don't know what pleasure means.'

'Perhaps pleasure, or happiness, means a bellyful of food, good clothes and comfortable sleep.'

Barota had crept in as they were talking. Noorabai was her latest victim. She butted in, 'Are you crazy? To have a voluptuous body and to indulge it with sensual fun and to enjoy oneself through it—that is what pleasure is. Didn't that pandit tell us that *raaslila* is the Lord's ultimate act in the world? Haven't you noticed how romantic it is during a *raaslila* and how it arouses everybody?' Barota's hands fumbled under Noora's sari.

The body gives me nothing—neither pleasure nor pain, thought Tapasi, remembering how she had hated it when Majumdar Babu had disrobed her and caressed her body every night. In the beginning she had felt some curiosity, followed by a strange tingling and shivering sensation, and then a frustrating blankness. Moshai Babu slapped and punched her and branded her with burning cigarette butts. He'd tried to cover his own physical inadequacy by laying the blame on her. For a long time she was unable to understand what was happening. The more Majumdar Babu thrashed her, the more hardened she grew till the sweeper woman explained to her, 'The master is a sick man. That is why he has bought you, Boi Di.'

'How do you know?'

'I've been working here for years. He once meddled with me and I learnt the secret right then. He pays me well and gives me gifts of saris so that I keep his secret. But how come you put up with such barbarity, Boi Di?' The sweeper woman's brazen laughter had shaken Tapasi.

MARIAM TAUGHT IN a school. She had a tiny room to herself in the Vidhwa Ashram for which she paid rent. There were lots of books in it. She left the grave like cell in the morning and came back laden with a heap of answer books to correct every afternoon. Mariam suffered from some kind of debilitating disease but Tapasi did not know what it was. However, they had taken to each other instinctively and Tapasi took care of Mariam whenever her condition deteriorated. Once, when Mariam was unwell, Tapasi checked all the answer books and realized with a pleasant surprise that she knew all the answers. She had not forgotten what she had been taught at school. Mariam and Tapasi would discuss books animatedly but Tapasi would grow quiet if she asked her anything about her past. Tapasi sometimes surreptitiously read books by the light of a lantern in Madam's room but she had to be careful. Ambika Devi kept an eagle eye on all her charges.

◆◆◆

It had rained that day and after it stopped everything around wore a melancholy look. The street leading to the temple was full of slush and the open gutters were overflowing with stinking dirty water. A couple of children were sailing paper boats. Their little paper boats would float or sink or get caught in the rubbish and stall. Tapasi watched them, engrossed in her own thoughts. She had no interest in sailing paper boats, nor did she wish to bathe in the rain, feeling the sharp drops of the pristine rainwater flow off her back. At any rate, the stern regulations and the punishing routine at the ashram prohibited such indulgences. She noticed the small earthworms that had appeared on the wet ground, which shrank into little circular forms when her feet touched them. Looking at them she wondered if like them, she too had some mechanism to protect herself from being trampled upon. Can I learn to shrink in self defence?

Further down the road a couple of rowdy boys had fastened a string to the claws of a pigeon. They first tossed the bird in the air and made it soar like a kite then brought it down, over and over, till the poor creature was half dead. Tapasi stopped and watched this act of cruelty intently. The boys then dug a hole in the ground and buried the fluttering, half dead pigeon in it before running noisily away. Tapasi ran with all her might, dug open the grave and rescued the pigeon, which was still breathing faintly. She wiped the bird with the pallu of her sari and gave it some water to drink. The pigeon got a second lease of life, the last day of its life had been extended into a continuum of it.

Insaf ka mandir hai yeh bhagwan ka ghar hai
Aana hai to aaja tujhe kis baat ka dar hai.
(This is the temple of justice where God resides
Come right in, you have nothing to fear).

◆◆◆

The evening *aarti* was coming to a close. It would soon be followed by another. The deep faith generated inside the temple was often reduced by the stench of urine and faeces that rose from the edge of the street. Temples have bells, holy echoes and incense. Churches have candles, flowers and their perfumes. Though everything is orderly and well regulated inside the temple, only a few elderly worshippers pray sincerely during the puja—the others either whisper to or stare at each other. Maybe they have no fear of God, nor belief in Him. The bhajan sequence goes on and on. The bhajans are not sung by people with hearts full of devotion, but by hapless, wretched people who have fallen on hard times. Wretches like Tapasi, Noorabai and Vrinda.

Tapasi was somewhat perplexed by the non-stop bhajan

singing. How come God isn't ever satisfied? Barota said she'd been here for seven years. How much more praise does this God made of stone want sung to him? And to what purpose? Tapasi was turning into Prashna, her questioning self, again. These moments of metamorphosis, of reverting to her questioning self, were not easy. Of course they were free of pain, but on nights when the questions attacked her, she couldn't sleep.

Tapasi confided her restlessness to Mariam who told her that there was something in her that was not allowing her to resign herself to a confined existence. That something was her consciousness, which existed independently of her and which could move away from and ahead of her body. That is why, inspired by it, man was able to transcend the body and contemplate higher things.

Ultimately, Tapasi decided that she had no right to change or violate the regulations of the ashram. Disturbing the system meant betrayal. And as far as she was concerned, she had always accepted her destiny. Whether she liked it or not, no untrodden path awaited her. If her past experiences were any indication, it was obvious that her journey ahead would also be painful.

◆◆◆

She had trusted Kanika Di and Jatin Da in Bolepur. Trusted them implicitly. She had tried to learn about the world through them. It was at their insistence that she had agreed to marry Majumdar Babu. She remembered Kanika Di's words: 'Majumdar Babu is a very nice person. He is rich and he has agreed to let you study further. For you, Tapasi, this marriage is like a door, a door leading to a staircase. You should take the stairs to go up otherwise that Kaka of yours will not spare you.'

Honouring the word of its elders was an age-old Bolepur tradition. The elders were like gurus, teachers, and guides—so there was no question of not following Kanika Di's advice. The great poet Rabindranath Tagore had lived near Bolepur and many of his noble ideas had originated in these lands. But Kanika Di, though born of the same lands, had not been inspired and had still pushed her into an abyss full of gloom and misery. Oppressed, she had discovered that money was more important than any noble idea or concept in the world.

Tapasi stayed awake during the nights pondering her ill-defined place in the world. She often felt that the dingy darkness of the smoky room was descending deep inside her to the extent that she was losing touch with all the lines and shapes of her past. In the morning, when she looked into space, her lustreless gaze would fall back on her like a recurring disease. Plus she felt light-headed. Her mind seemed to wander in an impenetrable labyrinth in which she grew more and more trapped and depressed.

Tapasi looked at the sun but did not see it. The crest of the temple, illumined and warmed by the sunshine, remained unperceived by her. When she peeped into the well she saw no reflection. Spells of dizziness left her reeling with helplessness. Sometimes she found herself wanting to plunge into it. Sometimes, it led her to go and hide in an obscure corner of the ashram. She was quite puzzled by her spells of dizziness, though she didn't mind them. She thought of them as an opiate for poor, weak and destitute people like herself. Blanking them out to pain.

Resting after an attack, she would think about her ramshackle bullock-cart standing under a huge tree outside Kaka's hovel. She had repaired the cart with coconut fronds, reeds and strings of jute fibre. Oh, how she loved sitting in it! Sitting in it and giving herself to such esoteric dreams! But now she had been declared as bare and broken as the bullock-cart had been when she had first found it.

Once again she took out her blue notebook and, by the light of the lantern in Mariam's room, wrote: 'Maybe my broken down bullock-cart will become whole again. Maybe it will even begin to move. I must make an effort in that direction. What should I do? Should I take the side of God or should I quit this enforced devotion to Him? I don't know why mute idols have been chasing me since my childhood. Why can't I exist without them?'

She stopped writing, wondering who would answer her questions. She was trapped in the narrow pathway of a stinking gulley where nothing was right, well-organized or acceptable to her. So what must I do? Fly away? She felt a compelling desire to fly across the sky. But then she came down, back to the realm of reality, where it was the time of *Prabhat Pheri* and she was on her way to the temple with Noorabai, Vrinda, Barota and Nanda.

◆◆◆

Their destination was a new temple situated in a different street tucked deep in the interior of Vrindavan. It was the temple of a God who incorporated all the paths to divinity.

The four of them were taking a new route. The novelty of the unfamiliar surroundings appealed to Tapasi. They were following a group of saffron-robed sanyasins some of whom carried single-string lutes and cymbals. Their clothes were dusty and a few of them were barefoot. They were singing a bhajan.

Mum priyatam ki madbu murli se gunjit tera vanvan upvan, jai, Vrindavan!

Mum priyatam ki madbu chitvan se viksit tera iarupaat suman, jai

The sanyasins were in an ecstasy induced either by the melody of the song or perhaps by religious fervour. Tapasi looked around at the squalid, narrow street littered with uncollected trash and the stinking drains full of stagnant dirty water. Pigs and mangy emaciated dogs foraged for food in garbage heaps full of dirty leaf plates and earthenware cups. The scene certainly did not inspire any feeling of sweetness and piety in her heart. So how come the sanyasins were so deeply stirred?

Presently, a magnificent temple came into view. As they drew close to it, one of her companions nudged her and said, Come on, Tapasi, let us go up. We have come to the temple of Sri Bankey Bihari.'

'Oh! have we?' Tapasi asked and started absently up the stairs.

'Hey you girl! Where are you going? The doors are closed. Bhagwan is still asleep. Just wait here. It'll be some time before the doors are open.' An impressive looking old man stopped them.

'All right. We'll wait here.'

Barota, Vrinda, Noorabai and Tapasi sat down to wait on the steps.

'Don't you think Bhagwan should rise early, Barota? He is God. How come he sleeps till late in the morning?' Tapasi could not resist asking.

By now the congregation of bhajan singers had also settled down on the steps. The impressive looking old man, in white clothes and with a white beard, overheard Tapasi's remark. 'Let me answer your question. Bhagwan Bankey Bihari Ji is an elegant, amorous, pleasure-seeking God. He spends the night in dalliance and this temple is the place where the lovers rendezvous. It often gets late by the time Bhagwan goes to bed after *raas*. Hence, it is not proper to disturb his sleep.'

'What is *raas*, Baba?' Tapasi asked, at which everybody burst out laughing and Baba turned his face away in embarrassment. Barota pinched Tapasi and whispered, 'Don't you know what *raas* is? *Raas* is what I practise all night.'

'*Chhi...you* always...' Tapasi left the sentence unfinished. Then turning to Baba she asked, 'Baba, if you don't mind could you tell me why this place is called Vrindavan? Also why is it believed to be sacred when it's so filthy?'

Baba was struck by the earnest look in Tapasi's eyes. He placed his hand on her head and said, 'Come, I'll tell you. According to the legends, Radhika Ji has sixteen names. One of them is Vrinda. This place is the playground of the one who bears the name Vrinda. That is why this place is so enchanting. Also, Tulsi plants sprout here of their own accord. That may be another reason for it being called Vrindavan. Another story says that after Sri Krishna fell in love with Radha he created Vrindavan in heaven. Subsequently, this place appeared on earth as a playground for them to cavort in, and since then, it has been called Vrindavan.'

Baba continued, 'Not just human beings but birds and animals too watch the winsome acts of Bhagwan with enchanted, wide-open eyes. Nature comes alive and becomes eloquent with an intoxicating sweetness here. Everything is geared towards pleasing the divine Lover and his Beloved. This town is awash with the love sent forth by the divine couple. The manifestation of their amour enlivens this place and bathes everything with joy. Yes, oh yes, that is Vrindavan.'

Baba seemed to be lost in an imaginary Vrindavan of his own description. But Tapasi was perplexed by the squalid streets, the bazaars where groves once existed, the beggarwomen, the blind and crippled folk. What a contrast between the actual place and Baba's description of it. What kind of contradiction was this?

Someone announced, 'Let us go in. The door has been opened.'

Pushed and jostled by the crowd, holding Vrinda's hand, Tapasi was somehow propelled into the temple. She could see that a priest dressed in yellow and green clothes had parted the curtains behind which the idols of the deities were placed and she caught a fleeting glimpse of the captivating face of the idol of Krishna with his beautiful, almond-shaped eyes and enchanting smile. His eyes were so animated that Tapasi felt she could hide nothing, absolutely nothing, from his penetrating gaze. She wanted to look into those eyes forever. Though she was mesmerized by the vision, which seemed to inspire her to go on living, there were far too many distractions. On one side the pandits were assisting the devotees with their offerings to the Lord. On the other, bhog was being made under a shower of flowers. A pandit was giving the bhog to the devotees in green and yellow plastic bags, who were also cupping their hands to take the *cbarnamrit*, the sacred liquid touched by the Lord's feet. Tapasi and her companions stood enthralled. Though they had nothing to offer they could at least watch the enchanting spectacle.

Abruptly, the curtain was jerked back and the Lord was once again screened away from His devotees. An irate voice rang loudly through the crowd, 'How come the curtain has been pulled so soon? These pandits don't allow the devotees to have a darshan of Bhagwan.'

'Don't blame the pandits. It is not their fault. Sri Bihari Ji's benevolence and love for his devotees is well known. On one occasion, an ardent devotee stared at him unblinkingly for so long that when he departed, Bihari Ji left the temple and followed him outside. It is believed that the pandit of the time had to implore Bihari Ji Maharaj to come back after which he was re-established in the temple with much ceremony. Since then, the curtain is pulled between him and the devotees after short intervals as a precautionary measure.'

Pushed and jostled by the crowd once again, Tapasi came out of the temple. Trying to sidestep the muck which spilled over from the open drains, Vrinda, Barota and Tapasi slipped and fell. They got up with great difficulty and began to walk through the narrow street with Barota spewing abuses. Vrinda stopped to buy something for her daughter, Chuniya. Tapasi had no money. Finally, after having gone through so much, she had begun to understand the importance of money and why people held onto it. She thought that they defined their existence through money and money helped them define their identity. Even religious faith could not be practised without money.

Ironically enough a blind beggar sitting by the roadside sang:

'Maya maha thagini, hum jaani.'

(I know that wealth is the biggest deceiver.)

She herself had stood in the temple like a pauper—no offerings, no incense sticks, no ceremonial grains of rice. She had brought nothing. She wondered how she was going to support herself, and also how she could worship God with no money in her pocket. She would have to find a way to rise above her penury. But how?

'Maya aisee mohini jete jive tele bhatkai.'

(Money is the enchantress that leads astray those who fall under her spell.) The song of the blind beggar buzzed around her like a poisonous wasp.

'Here, take the prasad and eat it.' Barota suddenly placed a *peda* in her hand. Tapasi wanted to eat it but the frustration of not being able to buy anything was so oppressive that she answered, 'No, I don't feel like it,' and gave the *peda* to a beggarwoman sitting nearby. 'I don't want to eat anything.' Her heart was heavy and she fought the unshed tears that threatened to spill from her eyes. She reminded herself that she was not going to break down—she would not resort to self-pity at her miserable state.

Walking swiftly, Tapasi reached the ashram and noticed that Baba, the old man she had spoken to at the temple, was talking to Ambika Devi. Tapasi was curious to know what they were talking about but she was scared of Ambika Devi. She went inside thinking about her own conversation with him. At least someone had considered her questions worthy of answers. Thoughts and ideas were like a screen covering her environment, as real as the silk curtain between her and Bankey Bihari. It was possible that the thoughts and ideas swirling inside her mind would settle if she could talk more to Baba.

◆◆◆

In time, Tapasi realized that Vrindavan had its own music, locked in its remote past. She wanted to capture that music for herself. She wished to hear for herself all that she had heard about—Sri Krishna standing under a kadamba tree and playing magical melodies on his flute; the birdsong out in the open sphere of Nature; the murmuring of the gently rippling waters of Kalindi; the cheerful laughter accompanied by the tinkling of the anklets of young maidens on the banks of the river or at the village well; the clinking of bangles and anklets as the mesmerized gopis moved towards Krishna playing languorous notes on his magical flute.

Brajbhoomi is believed to be steeped in the synchronized music of all these sounds. The intoxicating sounds rising from this sacred earth were not worldly because one did not hear the strains of the material world in them. But where has all that music gone from Vrindavan today? How come the crude din of the material world is so powerful that it has even drowned the music of sacred places?

The ambience of the holy places—the teerthas—is different from the rest of the world. Their music, temple dances and smells lend them a different colour all together. The fragrance rising from the lighted oil lamps, the perfume of flowers and joss sticks and the *samagri* smouldering in the *havan* vessels, all combine to give these places a characteristic aroma. It is ironical that their fragrance, which should lead to God, has instead been reduced to the furthering of corporeal pursuits. It is generally observed that man finds contrariety attractive. Means are means and their use depends on man's mentality. The mantras, which once were deemed immortal, are now reduced to the weak whispers of dejected and helpless people or have been corrupted into the tunes of popular film songs. The dances too have become filmi and bhajans have been reduced to versification devoid of sentiment and meaning. Even the Gangajal and *charnamrit* have not been spared. They have been replaced by opium, toddy, hemp and other substances routinely abused in the temples. Does the pristine practice of religion exist at all?

Earlier, religious rituals were imbued with deep feeling. They were beautiful—a vehicle to spirituality. Meditation, worship, rituals of worship—all have been reduced to gestures and lip service.

Then there are these poor widows with scarcely any resources—physical, emotional or financial. They too are being experimented with. Six hours of jaap in the temple, two rotis and two dhotis. That is the sum of their existence. And the pandits? All busy experimenting too. Ringing brass bells and sounding gongs. Making their own din—the sound of authority and of fear. Adding to the raucous clamour of holy places. It is an inner fear that brings people to places of pilgrimage. Fear is the feeling behind these rituals of worship, offerings and *aartis* which grow steadily in number every year. You can hear different kinds of bhajans and *chaalisa* prayers all around. The number of chants and the number of devotees has increased manifold. Oil lamps, joss sticks, camphor, the multi-flamed sacred fire. The numbers keep increasing. Along with them, the ostentation has grown too. There is a marked increase in the quantities of prasad flowers and sticky *charnamrit* dripping on people's feet. Shoving and pushing crowds, regulated, limited-time darshans of Bankey Bihari, devotees being pushed and jostled, hands groping, grabbing and fondling private parts. Organized systems and regulations have overtaken true religious sentiment. The devotees are held in check with cordons and ropes.

The yellow and orange robes of the pandits, their raucous voices spouting expletives, the police lathis, all lead to an arrangement devoid of sentiment. Who chants the mantras? It is said that in the sanctum sanctorum of a temple, a mantra is chanted at all times of night and day, a mahamantra which is an ongoing echo in the very air of that place. Does anybody know what mantra it is? Experimentation there, too. Some mantras are earmarked to help accomplish your work, some tantrik mantras are designated to solve problems. Does it mean that religion is just a play of words towards ones selfish gains?

Tapasi had been told that mantras were a manifestation of man's love for God. They were not only pleasant but powerful sounds which revealed hidden feelings, and once expressed, floated in the atmosphere for ever to save it from being corrupted. Tapasi, Noorabai and Vrinda were forced to sing bhajans though they hadn't a clue what bhakti was all about. They were not enamoured by the mystique of these places. For them, the mantras and bhajans sung in indistinct notes and a corrupted language were merely a means of survival. Two rotis and two saris. Did it mean that these aspects of worship were mere rituals peculiar to a teertha, or practices they had to follow whether they liked them or not? At any rate, poor widows like them were too weak and helpless to swim against the tide.

In addition to the music, dance, fragrances, flowers,

offerings and mantras, the holy teerthas were also imbued with a certain mystique of their own. Almost all of them were reached after difficult journeys. The hazardous journeys were an indication that the pathway to God was not easy. But today, after braving the arduous journey, when one is finally in viewing distance of the propitiated God, there are fluttering silk curtains between the seeker and the sought. And all sorts of curious things and unusual characters. Such as the androgynous woman who was often seen dancing bizarrely on the platform outside the temple. She was dancing that day too. The crowd of spectators clapped and laughed and made crude remarks about her. She was dancing and singing all by herself.

'Pag ghunghroo bandh Meera nachi rey
Hai, Meera nachi rey.'

Her style of clapping and her dance were as crude as her singing. An idol of the lord in an intricate pose of classical dance was enshrined inside the temple, while outside one was subjected to this vulgar performance, mused Tapasi, as she craned her neck to get a good look at the dancer. She noticed that the dancer's figure was very different from other women like Noorabai or Vrinda. But the dancer was totally absorbed in her performance and looked as if she had been transported to another world.

Tapasi then began to wonder why the Lord was depicted in an attitude of dance inside the temple. Was it because the whole cosmos was dancing to his rhythm? She remembered that she had danced on only one occasion, at Kanika Di's house. And as she danced she too had become oblivious to everything around her. Was it the effect of the rhythm of the dance or the presence of Malay, Kanika Di's handsome son, that had created such ecstasy in her? What an unprecedented joy she had felt. A thousand tiny silver bells still clinked through her body when she thought back to that moment. Perhaps Meerabai had experienced the same feeling—only much more intensely. That is why, oblivious to herself, Meerabai went dancing around the groves and alleys of Vrindavan singing the splendour of Krishna.

Tapasi wondered if the tuneless song, the ugly face and the ungainly male figure of the present dancer was not a mockery of Meera's unparalleled adoration of him.

'Do you know how she became a eunuch?' Panditji asked Tapasi as he handed a paper cone full of prasad to the dancing Devdasi.

'No,I don't,' Tapasi answered, and put down the cymbals. 'Long ago, a great sage, a visionary, lived in Vrindavan. He used to go begging for alms to Madhukari, where an affluent family gave him food and other things everyday. There was a newly-wed daughter-in-law in the house. As she was giving him food one day, she brushed her big toe against the foot of the sage, who took no notice of it. But when the new bride played the same mischief on the second and third day, the sage stood on the threshold of the house and said loud and clear, "I shall not come here again. You have come here to corrupt the young men of this place." The in-laws of the new bride implored him for forgiveness but she died the same day. Since then, she gets reborn as a eunuch over and over again.'

'*Radhey, Radhey*,' Tapasi muttered and trembled in fear. Then she asked, 'Swamiji, will she ever be set free from that curse?'

'Yes, she will when the time comes.'

'And when will that be?'

'How do I know? You are always asking questions. So many questions, all the time! What is your name? Tapasi?' Looking annoyed, Panditji left the place.

A couple of urchins started to lob stones at the dancing eunuch. One of them hit her on the forehead. Blood trickled down her face—fresh, deep red blood. Her tuneless bhajan wavered and her dance slowed down but she did not stop.

Sri Krishna sharnam mum....

Her song seemed to emanate not from her mouth but from her soul. The blood oozing from her forehead dripped onto her sari. Abruptly she stopped, and looking around manically began to run. Tapasi felt strange—as if an unseasonal dark cloud was rising inside her. She too wished to flee and escape the reality of her life in the ashram—a reality steeped in desolation. She desperately wished for some solitude, a quiet place to calm herself down.

Tapasi had read the name tattooed on the eunuch's arm before she'd disappeared. Devdasi. Her mind was deeply disturbed by the image of her bloodied face. Watching the flies buzz around the gash on the eunuch's head reminded her of the hungry, emaciated children and naked, shrivelled-up women of Somalia. The image of the urchins throwing stones at Devdasi was now superimposed on the images of the starving kids of Somalia. It is utterly insane. What is happening to the world? How come one is surrounded by squalor and cruelty everywhere? Flies swarming on heaps of trash. Flies hovering over the Devdasi's bloodstained face. Then, out of the blue, memories of yet another day flooded her mind.

One day in Bolepur she'd discovered bloodstains on her sari. The stains were caused by blood trickling down between her legs. Utterly confused and frightened, she had rushed to Kanika Di who glared at her and said, 'You are crazy. Such a big girl and you don't even know what this is! You have grown up, Tapasi. Every girl grows up like this.' On that day, Tapasi understood that childhood was a stage she had crossed. She had come of age. She also remembered something else that Didi told her. 'Don't let Kaka know about this, otherwise he will sell you off in Sonagachhi—like he sold your mother.'

'Sonagachhi? What is Sonagachhi, Didi?'

'Run off now. I'll tell you some other time.' Tapasi had no wish to run off but she did what she was told and left without getting an answer to her question. The fear of growing up had begun to creep insidiously into her mind. Her gait was no longer as nimble as it was before 'the change' had occurred in her body.

Tapasi's mind had a way of shooting in different directions all at once. She would think about one thing now, ponder something else, then dive deep into something totally different before rising to the surface again.

◆◆◆

Vrindavan was preparing for Janamashtmi. The streets were chock-a-block with festoons, leaf garlands, flowers and buntings. Policemen bustled about making arrangements. Temple officials drew up all kinds of elaborate plans. New finery and floral decorations were being arranged for the Lord. It was a special occasion with special ceremonies and pujas. All the visitors to the town had also suddenly become devotees. Families arrived from far-off places: sadhus, sages, mendicants, thieves, burglars, all added to the throngs around the temples. Were they all driven by religious fervour and ardent spirituality? Innumerable faces dissolved into each other. Rope strings, police batons, orders being screamed, rising piles of filth in the street, mud, slush, mangy dogs. Do we call this celebration? Tapasi wondered.

Every now and then, one could hear cries of, 'Give way, clear the crowd, give way!' and a prosperous party of devotees would push itself ahead. 'He is a big moneylender,' someone would explain. Then the voices of protest, 'So what if he is a bigshot? We are all equal inside a temple. A temple is the abode of God. It is the house of justice.'

'Why do these people come here?' Tapasi could not keep herself from asking. She was playing the cymbals.

'Some people come here just to show off, others come to make offerings. Then there are those who come to watch the show and still others who only come to press themselves against the curvaceous bodies of the women in the crowd—maybe to touch and fondle them! Oh, what a great sensation it is to press against them! Where do you find the faithful in this age? It is Kaliyuga, the age of darkness,' said a man leering at her, even as another shoved himself forward saying, 'Let me go. I came here before you.'

'No, I won't let you go before me. I'll go in first. I'll do the darshan first.'

An altercation followed. A babble of voices began to claim their right to go in first.

Within a few moments, the pushy man had stuffed a few crumpled currency notes into the hand of the presiding pandit. He was heard saying, 'Give me prasad, do the tilak, tie the sacred thread on my wrist first. I have made such a rich offering.'

The priest shot his arm out, picked a garland from the idol and threw it round the man's neck. After applying a vermilion tilak on his forehead, he tied a red string around the rich man's wrist and handed him an orange plastic bag with a coconut and some cut fruit. Tapasi was asked to help the priest conduct his job and she could not restrain herself from asking, 'Baba, why is tilak applied to people? What does the red mark on your forehead and also on the forehead of the other pandit signify?'

'A tilak is applied on the forehead because it is the most sensitive part of the body. The centre of the forehead is the site of the third eye. A tilak applied there stimulates the third eye and reminds you that you have to open it to really see the world. And that is possible only when the good deeds of several births bring you to the point where you gain enlightenment. This reddish orange dot is a door, a mark of resolution which we have to make with our life.'

Though the people were supposed to have been deep in meditation, most of them were busy pushing and jostling each other and endeavouring to move forward. The oil lamps were alight and the *aarti* was in progress. Hoping to transfer some of the piety of the idol to the populace, flowers and garlands from the Lord's idol were draped around the necks of the men and women. There was a confluence of diverse images all around. Tilaks on foreheads, mouths devouring sweets, hands clasped together, hands parted, hands caressing, expressive of the language of touch, eyes watching, searching, glaring, moistening with tears, eyes squeezed shut, voices issuing forth expletives, voices hissing, calling out or transforming into the rhythm of a bhajan. All these phenomena rise from the physical body and are integral to it. So, then, what is this thing called 'self?' Ego? Is it meant to be carried along with us when we die or must it be separated from us and left behind at home? The idols of deities are not their bodies. They are only symbols. But if the Gods behind the idols are real, do they have their egos? Right now, their 'self' was in the hands of the pandits who were exploiting it to the hilt. All these prayers and this ritualistic worship were an effort to get close to the Lord and to connect with him. But do we connect at all? Do these mercenaries allow us to gain proximity to God?

The door of the temple was finally closed. Maybe the Lord was also tired. Vrinda was slinking away quietly with some stolen fruits and sweets in a cloth bag. Her inner self was engraved with one single image, an image she could never shake from her consciousness—that of her afflicted child, her crippled daughter, Chuniya, who dragged herself along with great difficulty on her poor bent legs. All feelings and sentiments began and ended with her. Her daughter was the centre of her existence. Vrinda was not committed to prayers or to the worship of the Lord. An idol is merely a resting place to a bird perched on top of it, and so it was for Vrinda. Tapasi wondered if to the crowd of worshippers with hands stretched out in supplication, to the widows, the sick and half dead men and women, these idols of the Lord were any more than a resting place, a perch.

There was no temple in that part of the narrow street and yet you could see a crowd. No idol, flowers, incense sticks or *aarti*—and still the place was teeming with people. Tapasi, Vrinda, Noorabai and Barota pushed through the crowd to see what was happening. Curiosity always attracts a crowd and a sense of wonder holds it together. They saw a man standing on a platform outside a dilapidated house. He was dressed in a shabby kurta pyjama and had a non-descript face but his voice was full of passion—almost explosively so. He held aloft a rolled up newspaper which he waved in the air like a baton. His face shone in the sun, perhaps with the radiance of confidence. His words flowed loud and clear:

'Ladies, Janamashtmi is a great day of celebration for you. Our government is trying to pass the Women's Reservation Bill! They have promised to give you thirty per cent rights. You must have seen prominent headlines of this news. Everything has been stated with such grandiose words. But have you read the fine print in the same newspapers? Little Naghma, age four years, raped behind a mound of earth. Her body was found in a men's toilet. People fighting for women's rights have apparently not been touched by this news item. Nor the one about the cold-blooded murder of an ailing sixty-year-old woman who lived alone in a barsati in Nizamuddin. The murderers had raped her before killing her.

'Do you think that the passing of this bill will alter the

conditions prevalent in our society? The body of a newborn girl child thrown in a garbage dump and baby girls strangled soon after birth are demanding an explanation of their life from you! Dying declarations of young women burnt for dowry seek an explanation of their plight everyday. Don't you realize that women are the worst enemies of women? They are the executioners who murder them.'

Vrinda began to sob and Noora gripped Tapasi's hand tight. Tapasi looked pale. Something seemed to burst within her.

'Who is killing women? Who is strangling newborn girl children? Who is raping little girls and even elderly women? Who is it?' The speaker addressed the crowd.

The men standing by scratched their groins. The women covered their heads with the pallus of their saris. Some mouths swore at the speaker who went on talking, oblivious to the reaction of the crowd.

'Do you realize how many problems you women have? Is there anybody who is trying to find solutions to your problems? Anybody at all? Let me tell you, nobody is interested in women's problems. The passing of this bill is just a cover-up for women's real problems! The bill is nothing but a colourful sheet of paper by which the custodians of the Constitution are trying to placate you. The government, temples, priests, even your families, are part of this conspiracy to dazzle your eyes so that you cannot understand their real motives. The reality you are not even aware of. The reality of your existence, your life, your being born a woman and the truth of your being human.'

The crowd fell silent. An eerie silence began to creep through it. The speaker continued, 'It is a fact of the life of each woman that she is a prisoner behind the doors of her house. She suffers violence at home and when she steps outside to demand her rights, she gets beaten up all over again. Roop Kunwar was killed behind the closed doors of her house and society declared her a sati after which they held massive celebrations of her death! Janamashtmi celebrations are held to delude you, to keep you oblivious to reality! So that you cannot understand what you should know. Don't you remember that a woman from these very villages was paraded naked in the city because she had dared to cross the threshold of her house and ask for police assistance to counter the goondas in her village? The police broke her legs because her daring and courage were intolerable to them. They believe that every thing is made for men. How dare a mere woman talk about her rights on the sacred soil of India? How dare she raise her voice? And to top it all, how dare she have the guts to fight a legal battle?'

The crowd had begun to get restive. '*Maro saale ko*!' By now the police had arrived and joined the throng. 'Look how he is provoking our simple womenfolk! *Saala*. He claims to be a journalist!'

The crowd was turning macho now. 'He is talking too much! *Ullu ka patha, saala harami* comrade! He is a comrade. *Maro saale ko*!'

A policeman took the speaker by the arm and tried to pull him off his pedestal. He shook his hand off and said, 'You are all used to listening to lies! You cannot take the truth! Let go of me! I work in a newspaper office! I'm not a comrade or any such thing!'

A few stout women came forward to intervene but the police dragged him away under a shower of lathis and expletives. He went with them, but did not stop shouting:

'You have no one, Sisters! All these custodians of the law and administration have sold their souls—the police, the legal agents, the court houses—none of them are for you. They won't support you! Don't expect any sympathy from them. You have to fight your battles yourself. Just reject these deceptions of Janamashtmi and all other rituals of worship. The Gods of today are all stone Gods. Why are you hitting your heads against stones? Come on, arise! This is the time to wake up, not to sleep!'

The crowd was dispersed with a lathicharge. Screams, confusion and stampedes followed. Tapasi, Vrinda, Noorabai and Barota managed to come out unscathed and they hurried on silently.

◆◆◆

The rooms of the ashram were bleak and gloomy. The only light was provided by a zero-powered bulb in the veranda, hopelessly ill-equipped to dispel the darkness of the interiors. Tapasi wondered why the darkness was so intense that night. It was so dense it almost seemed clotted. There were layers upon layers of darkness. Does darkness have layers? Can't we tie it in bundles and chuck it out of the window? Where was the sun? Why was it necessary for it to fade and disappear every evening?

Vrinda jumped out of the window and disappeared into the outer darkness of the street. The gloom inside the ashram, intensified by the dim light of the veranda, grew more oppressive with the feeble whimpers of Vrinda's daughter. Tapasi wondered what to do to soothe her. She had nothing to offer her. No milk, no food, no toys. Should I let her cry? What else can I do? After all, the water in the unwashed glass is just water and nothing else.

NOBODY IN THE ashram knew for certain what Ambika Devi's real name was. Her entire existence, or so she claimed, was devoted to the welfare of the downtrodden, to the widows, who, after being discarded by their families, had taken shelter in the ashram under her protection. She had received a number of awards and citations, which duly framed, were displayed prominently on a wall in her office. A flattering close up of her shiny, smiling visage on the wall added to her stature.

But there was no one about whose history and background Barota did not find out sooner or later and it was she who revealed that Behenji—as Ambika Devi was called by the inmates of the ashram—belonged to a small mofussil town, Etah or maybe Bhadoi. When she was young she used to dress like a film star. She married early. Her husband owned a good English medicine store with the word 'Chemist' on the signboard. After she was married, Ambika Devi sometimes minded the store. Her knowledge about the drugs she sold was enhanced by reading medical prescriptions. Whenever her husband went to Delhi or Agra to purchase supplies, she took care of the shop with great efficiency. Her dress, hairstyle and mannerisms attracted a lot of customers and business grew by leaps and bounds.

Dr Yadav also came by sometimes, driving his vintage Ford to the shop. He was the superintendent of the only hospital in town. In his time, he had studied medicine in Kota on a seat reserved for schedule-class candidates. It was a small town with just one hospital so he enjoyed not only an important, but also a powerful position. Like a snake who sloughs off its old skin, Dr Yadav had abandoned his legally wedded wife and sent her off to an obscure place where she was probably reduced to working as a menial in some home or as a farmhand on the fields. It was at this stage in his life that Dr Yadav met Ambika Devi and was as attracted by her awesome personality, as she was by his flashy, second-hand car. A romantic exchange of medicines began to take place, not only in the shop but also in the compound of the hospital. A lot of medicines and hospital equipment were ordered from the shop, leading to Ambika Devi's greater involvement with him and to the success of her business. Anyway, irrespective of how they begin, all circles end at the same point. Life and its upheavals move together. Dr Yadav obtained a transfer and joined a hospital in Vrindavan where he arrived driving his fancy Ford with Ambika Devi by his side. Ambika Devi's husband raised a hue and cry, running from pillar to post, but Dr Yadav was obviously at an advantage and so the former lost out to him. Soon enough, two sons were born to Ambika Devi and him, which sealed their union, legitimate or otherwise, it didn't matter.

All these exciting events had taken place a long time ago. Time and change always march together. The sons grew up and lost interest in Vrindavan. Inspired by his mother's unfulfilled desires, one of them went off to Mumbai to become a film hero. The other was studying in a college in Gwalior.

Ambika Devi enjoyed the good life for a few years after which Dr Yadav suffered a paralytic stroke. The right side of his body was paralysed. After going through something of a financial crisis, Ambika Devi found employment at the Sri Radha Krishna Vidhwa Ashram, which had been founded by a rich man from Mumbai. He entrusted her with the total administration of the place. Though she received a regular salary she also made a lot of money on the side. Consequently, within a few years, her single-storeyed house acquired another floor. The top floor was rented out. A widow from the ashram was dispatched to work as caregiver to Dr Yadav as well as to run the household. Dr Yadav was confined to a wheelchair. Frustrated by his distorted face and twisted arm and leg, he had fallen prey to depression and kept mostly to his room. Ambika Devi treated him shabbily. She had grown ill-tempered and foul-mouthed living in her environs. That is why she picked up a stick and screamed at everyone as soon as she reached her office everyday. She had no qualms about bringing down her stick on a widow every now and then. Everyone feared her.

Tapasi often wondered whether there was anybody in the world who was totally free from fear. She herself was scared of Barota's conduct in the ashram. Vrinda was scared of her daughter's inability to walk, Noorabai of hunger, Bhagwati of being thrashed. Eveyone lived with some fear or the other. None of them were completely strong in themselves. But what about Ambika Devi? Why did her voice always quaver? Why was she always scared? What was her fear? The fear of being exposed in front of the women? Or the fear of being dismissed from her job?

One day, Mariam and Tapasi were summoned by her. On reaching her office they found Ambika Devi ashen-faced, holding a letter in her trembling hand. Mariam read the letter first and then passed it on to Tapasi. Tapasi wanted to laugh out loud on reading the letter but she restrained herself when she looked at Ambika Devi's pale face. The letter went as follows:

> 'A priest was performing puja in a temple at Singpur when a snake made a sudden appearance. The priest was scared out of his wits. The Snake-God transformed himself into a Brahmin and said, "Fear not, but listen to me carefully. I'll be reincarnated on earth in a short while and exterminate those who destroy dharma. Whoever prints and distributes a thousand leaflets in my name will have his/her wishes fulfilled in 24 days. Those who fail to do so within 24 days will suffer major losses."

Saying this the Snake-God in the garb of a Brahmin moved back three paces and vanished.

'After hearing about this incident, a man from Mumbai distributed a thousand leaflets and won a lottery for Rs 62 lakhs. A rickshaw-puller of Dhanbad distributed 650 leaflets and discovered a pot of gold in his house. Similarly, a man merely thinking about printing them, got a good job, after which he printed and distributed a thousand handbills. Another man dismissed it as a lie and his son died. Babulal Gupta of Agra received a handbill but he did nothing about it for a month. As a consequence he suffered massive losses in his business and also lost his wife. You should have faith in this miracle and spread the tidings about Shankarji amongst people. Whosoever receives this leaflet is requested to reprint and distribute a thousand copies. Do not risk disaster by dismissing it as falsehood. Instead, avail of the benefit brought about by the blessings of this miracle.'

The letter did not have the sender's name or address but Ambika Devi was simply petrified. Mariam tried to calmly explain the phenomenon of chain-mails to her but Ambika raged, 'You are a Christian! What do you know about Shankar Baba's wrath or his benedictions? Anyway, both of you are educated and can write. Please make 650 copies of this letter. I'll be in a state of mortal fear till they are sent out.'

You can't argue with someone who is armed with a cane. Tapasi and Mariam worked day and night for four days and made the required copies of the letter. They were sent to all the addresses listed in the office register and to other addresses that Ambika Devi gave. When the work was accomplished, a grateful Ambika Devi surreptitiously rewarded them ten rupees each for the first time in her life. But even then she was not completely free from anxiety. She picked up a copy of the letter and said to Tapasi, 'Come with me to Govardhan. A very wise baba lives there. Let us go to him and get the mystery behind this letter unravelled.'

Tapasi was convinced that the letter was utterly absurd but Ambika Devi was not about to agree with her. In any case, who was she to explain things to her? Moreover, she did not want to miss an opportunity to get out of the ashram. She quickly washed her face and stepped outside. Ambika Devi had already engaged a rickshaw and they both climbed in. This time they were moving away from the town. Tapasi could recognize a few streets.

By now, she had effected a compromise of sorts with her circumstances. Her companionship with Mariam and her books were helping Tapasi find some moorings. The life-denying environs of the ashram were like an experiment or a penance through which she was unearthing one deep truth or the other. At length she said, 'Don't be afraid, Behenji. No harm will come to you. As it is, so many letters have been sent. Everything will be fine.'

'Yes, I hope so. May the Lord bless us. I was really scared. As it is, Doctor Sahib is in poor health and the boys are not employed yet. I am the sole breadwinner of the family. *Radhey, Radhey*. I was really scared. You are so innocent, Tapasi. How can I make you understand how things work here? The mahants and sadhu babas of the muths in Vrindavan are really wily creatures. They have their musclemen. A whole sinister network operates here in the name of discipline. They indulge in all kinds of underground activities. Drugs—hashish ganja, opium—illegal arms, all these things. They murder in broad daylight and commit all sorts of crimes behind their saffron robes. They think nothing of raping women. Who knows, even this letter maybe an act to cause harassment to us. They have a whole army of goons at their beck and call. But what do I have? I have you girls. I have protected all of you so far. I've not supplied a single girl to any of them. God only knows what is going to happen.'

Tapasi was flabbergasted. 'Do such things really happen in the world, Behenji?' she asked, trembling with fear.

'Yes, they do. About five or six months ago, Mahant Charudutt took a fancy to the wife of Onkarnath, an official in a local muth. He demanded point blank that the woman be handed to him but Onkarnath refused. Mahant Charudutt took some goondas with him and while they kept a watch he murdered Onkarnath in broad daylight—after raping his wife in front of him. Nobody said a word. Not only did they vandalize the muth, they walked away with a lot of cash and looted goods. Mahant Charudutt is now absconding and the woman is missing. His goondas are taking care of the muth. A police case had been registered but the police officials are in cahoots with the culprits, instead of carrying out investigations. What is the use of filing a case, anyway? The Mahants, Pandas and Babas are least bothered about the incident. No one can arrest the offenders.'

Tapasi listened in rapt attention. She was aghast that such shocking incidents happened on the same sacred ground whose soil had been consecrated by the feet of the Lord and whose air was vibrant with the memory of the honeyed melodies emanating from His flute.

The rickshaw-puller too had been listening to their conversation. He chipped in, '*Arrey*, Behenji, how to tell you this, but bad characters, murderers and criminals absconding from big cities find shelter in these very muths. I ferry them in this very rickshaw so often.'

'I know that,' said Ambika Devi. 'I remember the police had once raided the place after being tipped that a criminal was hiding in Phatuta muth but the presiding Mahant had opened fire on the police and killed a constable. The Mahant was kept in the lock-up for two or three days and then set free after a rich seth furnished bail for him. *Arrey* Behenji, he is still holding his position at the muth. He enjoys great authority there. Last year, I took a gentleman passenger from the railway station to the muth of Kalikamliwale Baba. He had two large trunks with him. They were so heavy that I sprained my back pulling them to the muth. The watchman of the muth told me that the trunks contained ganja, hashish and opium. Well, I really don't know if it was true but since that day I have sworn never to take passengers from the railway station. By *Radhey Maiya*, I'd rather eat less than be a partner in crime.

'This reminds me of a recent news item in the papers. Apparently a man disguised himself as a sadhu in order to sell ganja in a city. He stuck a trident in front of his residence and inside he had this peculiar idol smeared with vermilion. He told the people who came for darshan that the idol gave off vermilion. Small pouches of vermilion were distributed as prasad. He claimed that his house was the temple of the thirteenth lingam of Shiva. Actually, he was supplying narcotics in the paper pouches. On festival melas, particularly on Shivratri, the idol shed a profusion of vermilion powder and a huge number of pouches were distributed. God knows whether he is in a lockup now or still at large and racketeering somewhere else.'

This was an eye-opener for Tapasi. So this was the reality of the teerthas, the pilgrimage sites of India and their great sages, pujaris and sanyasis. Was this really the hallowed land where Lord Krishna had been born? The dust rising from the unpaved road settled on Tapasi's body. The vermilion powder mixed with sweat from her forehead was streaking down Ambika Devi's nose. It was hot and dusty and the path was uneven and bumpy. Not a trace of greenery could be seen anywhere. Where had all the Kadamba trees, under which Krishna played his flute, gone? And those verdant gardens and meadows where the cows of Braj went to graze? Nothing remotely of the sort came into view. All one could see was a half-built town, piles of trash, spires of dust rising in the wind and occasional pools of stinking, stagnant water.

Presently they came upon a group of people dressed mostly in rags, walking barefoot on the hot ground. Some of them sang bhajans, the others were chanting something and rolling their bodies on the ground, dragging themselves along with the others in the group. They carried pebbles with them and placed one ahead of them to which they would stretch out their arms. Once there, they would stand up, mark it with their fingers and lie down again to roll and drag themselves further. Tapasi could not help asking Ambika Devi what they were trying to achieve.

'Don't you know, Tapasi? They are making a *parikrama*, circumambulating Govardhan Parvat.'

'What does *parikrama* mean, Behenji?' Tapasi asked her next question with some trepidation.

Ambika Devi was in a better mood now so she replied

kindly, 'You are so naive, Tapasi. Don't you know that Goverdhan is king of the mountains. Sri Krishna had lifted it and held it aloft on his little finger for seven days to protect the people of Braj from torrential rain. The people of Braj revere this hillock like a God who fulfills the wishes of everyone. Once their prayers are answered, the devotees perform the *parikrama* a second time in thanksgiving. Very often, these journeys are undertaken either on a full moon night or on a moonless one. This is a mountain abundantly blessed. The touch of the Lord is still warm in each atom of this place.'

Tapasi was really naive. She looked far and wide but saw nothing remotely like a mountain as far as her eyes could see. 'But I do not see anything like a mountain here! Where is Giriraj Goverdhan?'

The rickshaw-puller was the one to answer her this time. 'It is *ghor kalyug*, the age of darkness, Behenji. That is why Giriraj is caving gradually into the earth. The earth is buckling under the weight of people's sins and misdeeds, you see. My father and grandfather told me how beautiful this place was in their time. The rocks here were tinged with blue. The footprints of Lord Krishna were imprinted everywhere. There were large and small caves where sadhus, sanyasis and mahants lived and meditated. This was the holy ground of penance which reverberated forever with the chanting of mantras. But now it is an abode of sin where the evil deeds of citizens have overpowered Giriraj.'

'Brother,' said Ambika Devi, 'according to Puranasi there is a curse on Sri Giriraj which is why it is slowly caving in. Anyway, it retains its glory even now. Mere physical contact with this place absolves you of all your sins.' Ambika Devi sat with her hands folded and spoke in a voice brimming with piety.

'Here, Behenji, we have come to the place of your Swamiji.' The rickshaw-puller stopped the rickshaw and the two women got off. Ambika Devi paid him and said turning to Tapasi, 'You will see how great this Swamiji is, Tapasi. He does not utter lies, he does not drink nor does he use drugs. He commits no violence.'

'Excuse me, Didi. Would you tell me what exactly it is that he does which makes him so great?' Tapasi could not keep quiet any more.

'He is a Mauni Baba, a silent sage. He has taken a vow of silence. He remains silent,' Ambika Devi answered. 'And now you too should stop prattling.'

They entered a spacious compound with a temple situated right in the centre. The temple of Uddhavji. They left their slippers outside and offered obeisance by touching the floor of the temple with their foreheads. Ambika Devi said, 'This is the only temple of Uddhavji in the whole of the Mathura and Vrindavan area. Do you know who Uddhav was? He was a friend of Lord Krishna.'

'Of course I know that,' Tapasi answered. 'After Sri Krishna went off to Mathura the gopis used to pester Uddhav for news about him. They complained to him and bared their broken hearts to him. He was the only person who shared their grief at being parted from Krishna.' She gazed into the large, stony eyes of the idol of Uddhav and recited,

'Nirgun kaun des ko vasi?
Madhukar kahi samujhai sonh de, boojhatisaanch na haansi
Ko hai janak, kaun hai janani, kaun nari, ko dasi
Kaiso baran, bhesb hai kaiso, kihi ras mein abhilashi?
Pavego puni kiyo aapno, jore karego gaansi
Sumat maun hwai rahyo bawro, Sur sabe mati nasi.'

After she finished reciting the poem by Surdas, Tapasi laughed, 'This is how the gopis challenged Uddhav and left him nonplussed.'

'*Arrey...* I did not know you were so learned!' Ambika Devi exclaimed and Tapasi immediately grew quiet. How remote her dream of studying and graduating from Vishwa Bharti appeared now. Tears rolled down her cheeks. But Ambika Devi was not one to pay heed to another's tears so she ignored Tapasi's and instructing her to proceed to Mauni Baba's place, began to stride ahead of her. But Tapasi was lost in the depths of the black, stony eyes of Uddhav as she pondered her own grief—a grief as solid and unchanging as the dark unblinking eyes on the face of the idol. And now that grief had begun to throb inside her heart though no echoes of it were heard. No one ever sensed it and no one had ever made an effort to relieve it. Would Mauni Baba?

Ambika Devi pulled out the letter from her bag and jotting down something on a separate piece of paper, handed it to the Baba. Tapasi wondered what she had written on the accompanying slip of paper. Baba perused both papers, wrote something on a slate and pushed it in front of Ambika Devi. This exchange of messages went on for a few moments. Then Tapasi stepped forward. She noticed a smile on the Baba's face. It was the smile of a man who knows and understands a lot. He had eyes that matched the smile—thoughtful eyes with a deep understanding. But why did he not speak? It is just as well that he didn't. Most people speak harsh words and are ready to quarrel at the slightest provocation. Maybe that was the reason behind Baba's silence. He was not misusing his gift of speech. He was focused on a contemplation of words. External silence is conducive to the working of the mind's inner processes. Tapasi wrote on the slate, 'Baba, why do you observe silence?'

'Silence is the best and most powerful communication. Silence does not enter the brain—it goes straight to the heart.'

'Does that mean that the creation of the spoken word

is useless? What is the utility of speech if sound is useless?'

'Sound is not useless but often words are extremely harsh and they can hurt grievously. Life flows gently on in silence and in the peace that silence brings, and moves spontaneously to the heart. Its impact is much greater than that of words.'

'Is this world going to exist in silence? Is it possible to survive in silence while living an active life?'

'The world exists in silence. You too are silent. You can see how worldly people have filled it with noise and confusion. Gather your energies about you, child. You will achieve much in life. Observe the truth with your eyes, contemplate with your mind. A habit of meditation is nascent in your being. Absorb yourself in that,' Baba wrote on a slip of paper which he handed to Tapasi. Tapasi accepted the note as if it was a priceless gift. It was something precious and exclusively for her. Baba motioned to Ambika Devi to step forward. 'This girl is extremely intelligent. Help her move forward. Do not put obstacles in her path,' he wrote on his slate.

Folding her hands, Ambika Devi looked from Baba to Tapasi. 'As you wish, Baba, as you wish.' She left Baba's room and Tapasi followed her, preoccupied with her thoughts. All of a sudden she noticed that they had come upon a small pond. It was a pucca pond built a long time ago. A culvert leading to the pond was inscribed with the words

'Aartigram' below which was a white marble slab engraved with the following sloka:

Goverdhan giran ramie radhakund priyam harre
Kartike bahulashtamyan tatra snatwa harre priya
Naro bhakto bhavodwepratisthithasya pratoshnam.

Tapasi copied the sloka on the margins of the slip of paper Baba had given her. Her treasure-trove was growing richer and richer. She did not know much Sanskrit though she wished to learn it. She knew Bengali and her knowledge of English was improving tremendously in Mariam's company.

'Let us go and take a dip in the Radhakund, Tapasi. It is said that all our sins will be washed away if we bathe there.' Ambika Devi seemed to have come prepared for a dip. She took out an old sari from her bag, changed into it and stepped into the pond. Tapasi did not have a change of clothes so she climbed down a few steps and and tried to dip her fingers into the scummy water. As it was, she had not till then been able to summon enough reverence to want to bathe in the black and green water. Besides, she was still overwhelmed by what Baba had written. Each second of her meeting with him, his words about meditation, were frozen in her mind.

Just then, a few men dressed like pandits started to move close to them. One of them opened a red file that looked like a ledger and asked Tapasi, 'Where have you come from? What is your *gotra*? Which city are you from? Who are your parents? Your address?' Tapasi moved away to escape their attention. When they persisted, she took courage in both her hands and countered, 'How does it concern you who I am?'

'*Arrey*, it is a part of our occupation. We keep accounts of generations of visitors to this place. Just answer our questions and we will produce records of several generations of your family. Are you a Hindu? A Brahmin?'

Tapasi grew anxious. All those questions seemed to target her identity. She felt as if the answers to all these questions would comprise the most significant aspects of her identity, as perhaps they did for each human being in the world. The identity of each individual is determined by a past, a history of generations. But she had no such history or tradition behind her. Her hands were empty and her existence devoid of meaning.

She was full of, and surrounded by, a kind of emptiness which kept her from identifying with the world around her. She was an object beyond description. What was she? Just a name ... a woman... a widow, with no past and no future.

'WHERE DO YOU keep going off to, Vrinda? Your daughter has been crying for such a long time.'

'What can I do, Tapasi? It is not as if I enjoy sneaking out. I go only for her sake. He gives me money and also milk for my Chuniya. Or else, how would I take care of her? Ambika Behenji does not allow me even one extra roti. There is no other support. Everybody wants my child to die but I am her mother, Tapasi. How can I let her die just like that? If my mother-in-law had not hit her with a pair of iron tongs, my child would not be a cripple today. She was born perfectly normal, Tapasi. But if you strike a two-month-old with a pair of iron tongs, she is bound to get grievously injured, and then who would get her treated? Her father died of drinking adulterated liquor soon after the incident. The bone in the child's leg could not be set right and she became lame. The doctor said that she could walk again after surgery but how can I afford such expensive treatment for her? Who will provide for her? Who will treat her?' Vrinda wept. Then wiping her tears, she started talking to Chuniya, 'Peer Baba says you'll be all right, my darling. Jyotishiji also predicts that you will be fine soon. Come, let me rub this medicated oil on your legs.'

She massaged the child's legs with total concentration.

After a while she spoke again. 'Do you know that Peepalwale Baba gave me this miracle oil today? He said my Chuniya will start walking in a month's time.'

'Has he given the oil for free? How much did you pay for it?' Barota taunted knowingly. 'Or did you sleep with him last night? I saw your window open.'

'Oh, she jumps out of the window every night,' Noorabai giggled. Then her mood changed in an instant and she asked Vrinda, 'Does Baba tell you other things also? Will he tell me where my Nanda and Mithu are?' Her eyes grew misty.

'Are you crazy?' Vrinda chided her, 'How can he tell you these things just like that? Do you have the children's horoscopes with you? He is extremely learned. He studies horoscopes. Lots of rich people come to him.' She poured a little oil onto the palm of her hand and began to rub it on her exposed breasts, which hung loosely from her frail body.

'The lines on the palms of my hands say nothing. Nothing at all. Whoever gets the horoscopes of poor, helpless women and their children made?' Noorabai sighed.

'What is a horoscope?' It was Tapasi's turn to ask.

'Oh! You don't know even that!' The women burst out laughing. By now Mariam had returned from school and joined them. She had heard the last bit of the conversation. A horoscope is a sheet of paper on which the time and date of birth, stars and planets are recorded. Pandits study it, make calculations and predict the ups and downs of the future of the people according to the position and movements of the planets and stars,' she explained gently to Tapasi.

'Oh, I see.' Tapasi grew pensive. A person like me, whose parents are untraceable, can never know her date of birth. So what am I to do? What pandit should I approach? She'd also heard that one went through a cycle of rebirths. 'From which birth is a horoscope made?' she asked, turning into Prashna, her questioning self, again.

The women laughed again at her query. Mariam explained, 'It is believed that there are thousands of births but you are born as a human being only once.'

'But how about this life in the ashram, living under such severe conditions imposed by others, doesn't this feel like a non-human life too?'

◆◆◆

Everyone had retired to bed. All was quiet and dark when suddenly there were loud shrieks of pain and terror from Vrinda's room. 'A snake—there is a snake here! It has bitten me and my Chuniya! Oh, we are going to die!'

Instantly lanterns were lit and everyone rushed to Vrinda's room.

'Where is the snake? How did it come here?' Someone asked.

'It comes every night.' Vrinda was trembling in terror. Stick in hand, Barota busied herself looking for the serpent in the nooks and crannies of the room.

'It comes everyday,' repeated Vrinda. 'Sometime as a snake and sometime as a ball of fire that tortures me. It spouts poison as it hisses. Yes, it spouts poison.'

Tapasi fetched a pail of water. She sprinkled some on Vrinda's face and offered her some to drink. 'Come to your senses, Vrinda. You are babbling. No one has come here! All the doors and windows are closed,' she said.

Vrinda opened her eyes, which had so far been squeezed shut. The door was open. There was a strong wind blowing outside. Suddenly the windows opened with a crash. The sound of the windows smashing together in the deep stillness of the night was creating an eerie effect. The others too were beginning to shrink in fear. They too got the uncanny feeling there had been someone in the room who'd jumped out of the window and disappeared into the darkness outside. It was the same window Vrinda jumped out of when she went on her nocturnal trips.

'He came through this window. It remains open all the time. I cannot sleep with the window closed. I'm sure he shut it after getting in. He had come to burn me. *Hai*...he is hell bent upon killing me!' Vrinda started howling again.

'What nonsense you talk!' Barota shouted.

'He does come,' Vrinda insisted. 'He comes in the form of a shadow and then turns into a squirrel. By the time he comes close to my body, he becomes a snake who hisses and spouts poison! Balls of fire issue forth from his mouth!

Oh, the wretch has scorched me completely! *Hai*...what will become of my Chuniya!'

Barota planted a resounding slap on Vrinda's face. Vrinda stopped howling at once and looked stunned. A deep silence descended on their pathetic world. Then Barota gave her a mouthful. 'You are creating such a ruckus in the middle of the night. Get lost, *saali*. The world won't miss you if you perish! Go, die and find deliverance from the misery of this birth! *Saali*, do you call this a life? Going "Chuniya, Chuniya" all the time! She is a lame child. Even if she lives, what kind of a life will she have? Ask your snake to come and bite this blighted being!'

'It is the ghost of my husband! He'll torment me, devour me, not his daughter....'

'Stop this nonsense! Your obsession with ghosts has ruined our sleep! If you don't shut up now, I'll set you on fire! Do you understand?'

Vrinda moaned once and then fell silent. She began to caress Chuniya's legs and locking herself into a stony silence, tried to go back to sleep. The others followed Barota out and went back to their beds.

Tapasi turned around to see them leave and thought that there was no difference between women like Barota, who walked about naked, and Vrinda who had no qualms about exposing herself and applying oil on her breasts in front of people. They were all alike in their pathetic nakedness. There was no privacy at the water tap where they bathed in the morning. She thought that nakedness was a complex form of fear. The whole environment in the ashram conveyed the message that the women and their bodies were alike. What was so uniquely special about individuals that needed to be covered? They had no right to feel shame, nor to cover their nakedness. Was this collective nakedness a kind of similarity, the anonymity of a uniformed group, or was it meant to humiliate?

Living in the ashram Tapasi had begun to feel dissociated from her body. As if something was trying to slip out of her body, but she did not know what it was. She often wondered whether Vrinda's astrologer and Mauni Baba—all those who had knowledge—had paved a special path for themselves, which they travelled. Did they undertake journeys just for the sake of walking? What should she do? Follow them or fly away like a bird? A bird's flight begins and ends without it leaving its footprints anywhere. Its journey is not determined by the maps in geography books. Tapasi wanted to take a journey like that.

◆◆◆

Madan Mohan Baba's muth was situated at the bottom of the long narrow street that went past the ashram. Madan Mohan Baba was a much revered man and you could often see large crowds around his place. His name figured in a large number of legends of glory and grandeur. Bhagwati recounted one of them:

'Madan Mohan Baba started as the temple attendant who guarded the shoes of the devout. On one occasion, a venerable sage removed his wooden sandals and said, "I'll be back shortly. Please take care of these." It took him two days to return from wherever he had gone. Madan Mohan Baba did not eat or drink for two days. He sat there day and night keeping a watch over the wooden sandals. Pleased with his dedication and piety the sage showered him with blessings. Madan Mohan Baba also devotedly served Sri Advaitacharyaji Maharaj who was from the family of Sri Chaitanya Mahaprabhu.'

That day a large crowd had gathered in front of the above-mentioned ashram. A big crowd usually means that something ominous has happened. People said that Baba was a hundred and ten years old, though his looks belied his age. It was reassuring to see him standing outside the temple. He was leaning on his walking stick looking stricken. Someone had died after all.

'Who's dead?'

'A devotee.'

Unhampered by the rain that had been pouring non-stop for days on end, an elaborate bier was being prepared with much fanfare. Driven by curiosity, Vrinda, Tapasi and Barota had accompanied Ambika Devi to the muth. Though someone had died, there was no air of mourning or grief where the people had gathered. It is not mandatory to weep when someone dies. Tapasi herself had not wept the day Majumdar Babu died. Only Vrinda was sobbing into the crumpled edge of her sari. Suddenly, a little boy appeared in the street. He jumped up and down clapping his hands and chanting, 'Baba's monkey has died! Baba's monkey has died!'

Several people in the crowd guffawed. Someone said, 'Are you crazy? Does anybody make such elaborate arrangements for the funeral of a monkey?'

But a disciple of Baba hushed the crowd and explained, 'You may not remember this, but a foreigner had come and sojourned in Baba's muth a few years ago. Remember the fair-skinned, blue-eyed devotee? He grew restless after three or four years and when he was packing up to leave, Baba told him in jest, "By leaving here, you are defying the orders of your guru. Son, you cannot achieve enlightenment if you wander around here and there like a monkey."

'But the Vilayati Babu had been born and brought up in a different culture. His *sanskaras* were such that he said insolently, "I've followed your orders and the discipline of this muth for long enough. Do you think I am going to do that all my life? I've been enlightened enough. I am sick and tired of the regimented life of your muth. I am quitting." Saying this he left the place and went away. For a long time nobody knew whether he was still in India or had gone to his own country. However, Baba used to miss him. One day, Baba was sitting in the courtyard and doing his meditation when all of a sudden a baby monkey came and clung to his feet. Baba realized instinctively that the monkey was none other than his disciple who had died and been reborn as a monkey. Baba fondly took him under his wing and showered him with affection. "Good you've come back. Do not go away now." Since then the deceased foreigner had been living with the Baba who named him Ramdas. Ramdas sat by Baba at every jaap and prayer. He would turn his face up and listen to everything withrapt attention. All the other disciples of Baba loved him too. At mealtimes he used to sit with the other diners and eat with perfect manners. Ramdas was found dead on the roof last night. He has achieved nirvana by Baba's grace.'

The monkey's bier was decorated with flowers. The funeral procession began to move slowly and grandly. Other sanyasis from the muth proclaimed, 'The soul is immortal' and 'The body decays but the soul lives on,' in loud and resonant voices as they walked along with the procession. It was quite unusual to hear these chants instead of the mandatory '*Ram naam satya hai*' and that too for a dead monkey.

Ramdas was consigned to the water in the Yamuna with the appropriate rites. Subsequently, the muth organized the ritual feeding of the poor. Vrinda went ahead and got food for her daughter. Tapasi contemplated the whole episode and came to the conclusion that the body, whether of man or of beast, was not as important as its deeds and *sanskaras*. Did that mean that her own body, which had been abused and brutalized by Majumdar Babu's impotent lust, had already perished? All at once, the bitter memories of torture and abuse she'd suffered at the hands of her husband began to scorch her body again, as if she was in a furnace and the raw nerves that, for a while had lain dormant inside her, began to throb and hurt afresh. The dead monkey was consigned to the waves of the Yamuna.

The torrential rain that had been pouring relentlessly for days, finally eased. The storm in Tapasi's mind subsided with it.

◆◆◆

Life remains smooth if everything works according to a set routine but a change in the regimen can make everything go topsy-turvy. It was an unusual morning at the ashram that day and the schedule of the Sri Radha Krishna Ashram had changed into a different kind of exercise. Instead of singing bhajans, the inmates of the ashram were busy carting goods out of the storeroom adjacent to the office. Cane in hand, Ambika Devi was keeping a close watch on them. She was a woman of little education who had no compunctions about speaking harshly to the women or even rapping them with her cane. Tapasi and Mariam took care of office accounts. The fact of their being educated was a permanent source of anxiety to Ambika Devi. Still, she did her best to maintain a strict discipline in the ashram.

Bhagwati and Vrinda were helping to bring in the goods from the storeroom. Tapasi was preparing an inventory of them. Five hundred blankets, two hundred saris, a hundred and fifty woollen shawls, steel utensils, tumblers, thaalis. A man dressed in a dhoti-kurta sat relaxed on a chair. He was making informal receipts on plain paper for the goods. Barota had fetched bottles of an orange drink for him and Ambika Devi. Vrinda was heard wheedling over and over, 'Please give me a blanket, Behenji. The one I have is in tatters. I shiver in it when I get fever at night.'

'You talk too much, Vrinda. I have allowed you to keep your crippled daughter with you. Is not that enough? I give you food, you have a roof over your head. On top of that I am well aware of your shady activities. Nothing is hidden from me. Now run off, otherwise, I'll whack you with this cane.' And sure enough she brought the cane down on her back with such ferocity that Vrinda would have fallen flat on her face had she not held onto the wall near her. Everyone was silenced by the impact of it.

The buying and selling session was soon over. Ambika Devi retired to the office where behind closed doors she sat counting the money she'd just made. The man who earlier sat on the chair was loading the merchandise onto a pushcart. A shaken Vrinda was going about her work on unsteady feet. The man surreptitiously handed a blanket to her. He chuckled lecherously and said, 'Here, take it and come over tomorrow night. This is my address.' He gave her a slip of paper and mounted his bicycle with a swagger, following the loaded pushcart with a triumphant smile on his dark and ugly face. Vrinda scooted off to hide the treasured acquisition.

After a while, Mariam and Tapasi were summoned to the office. Ambika Devi had changed her sari and sat like the heroine of a Hindi movie, a la Rekha, with a big red bindi on her forehead. She held a bulky bag in her hands.

She took off her large, gold-rimmed spectacles and retouched the make up on her swarthy face. At length, she addressed Tapasi and Mariam:

'Listen, both of you. You are not to mention a word about these goods or about the money and accounts relating to them, understand? Come with me, Mariam. Let us go to the bank and deposit this cash. It'll come in handy if we have an emergency here. What is money to me? I have committed myself to the service of you all. I, my whole life, my very being, all that I have, is dedicated to the cause of social service.' Ambika Devi philanthropically presented them with a blanket and fifty rupees each and resumed her monologue. 'Keep them. They are for you. I want to keep you happy. Do you get me?' Her eyes glinted.

'I am already late for school, Behenji. Exams are on nowadays. Please excuse me and take Tapasi with you instead. She has had a better education than me. She'll take care of everything,' Mariam said.

'Actually, I could have managed on my own. But come with me, Tapasi. I'm just a trustee of this money which belongs to all of you. None of it is mine. Oh yes, Tapasi, go and put on a clean sari. My ashram gets a bad name when its inmates dress in dirty clothes.'

'I'll be back in a moment,' Tapasi said and left the office with Mariam. As she changed her sari, she said, 'How hollow Ambika Devi's proclamations of I, me and mine sound! She indulges in hypocrisy and dishonesty in the name of service.'

'You are right, Tapasi,' Mariam replied. 'Her behaviour reminds me of what I read once about a dramatist who died in an accident. The owner of the company for which he worked was hit hard by his death because he incurred huge financial losses. At the funeral, just before the coffin of the deceased was lowered into the grave, he paid his tribute in the following words, "I employed him when he was in dire straits. I staged his plays, honed his skills as an actor and helped him become such a great artist. I am the one who got his books published. I am responsible for all the awards he won and the fame he achieved..." He was still holding forth when the lid of the coffin flew open and the dead man stood up saying, "Excuse me, sir. Whose funeral is it, yours or mine?"'

Tapasi burst out laughing. 'Even a dead man could not stand the clamour of "I, me and mine". He stood up even though he was dead!'

'A man has two voices in him—one of self-love and the other of universal love. The emphasis on self-love is muted in those who are swayed by a love for all.'

'Ambika Devi does not love anyone. Who cares for others, anyway? It is all a sham we are putting up with.'

'Come on, let us make a move now, otherwise a couple of strokes from her cane will demolish all talk of love.'

She folded the currency notes Ambika Devi had given her and hid them in her blue notebook.

Tapasi came out and stepped into a rickshaw with Ambika Devi. She loved riding in rickshaws. Being driven by someone else was a novel experience and so was taking a new route. They were travelling a route different from the one they took to the temple everyday. Ambika Devi gave directions to the rickshaw-puller: 'There is a mound of earth beyond the turn ahead of Venue Koop—the Dwadashaditya Tila. Take us there. The large building in front of the Tila is the bank.'

The rickshaw-puller turned right and reached the mound of earth but there was a huge crowd on the road beside it. A man dressed in a dhoti-kurta and wearing a jacket stood on the mound. He was light-skinned and his eyes were bright with excitement. He looked familiar to Tapasi and when he waved his hands in the air and his voice reached her, she recognized him.

'Even after fifty years of freedom we are still in bondage! We are slaves who are bought for votes! Someone or the other always rules over us. First, it was the British and now a set of illiterate, selfish bandits who go by the name of political leaders! Our integrity and autonomy have been crippled by their wily politics! At each election, these crafty leaders of ours dazzle us with rainbow dreams, offer some nourishment to our starving selves, toss us a sheet to cover our nakedness and rob us of our conscience! They make grand promises of houses instead of footpaths for all! We take them at their word and start chasing the dreams they weave for us. But the moment they assume power they become oblivious to the importance of our votes and our very existence! Ultimately, what do we get? We get the same life of deprivation—fire in the belly, rags to cover the body, hands stretched out to beg for food....'

Ambika Devi got off the rickshaw cursing the man. 'The wretch is criticizing the leaders of the nation. Just look at his guts! He is provoking all those poor beggars. What will he achieve through such talk? He'll learn his lesson when the police catch him and beat him up. He gets beaten up ever so often but simply refuses to stop the nonsense he utters. Let us move fast, Tapasi. We'll hurry and finish our work in the bank quickly. We'll be caught in the crowd if violence erupts here.' She tugged at Tapasi's arm and hurried towards the bank.

It was Tapasi's first visit to a bank. She had not even known that such an institution existed. She studied all the signboards and read all the names before Ambika Devi instructed her how to deposit the cash. She went to the appropriate counter, filled up the deposit form, and got Ambika Devi's signature on it.

'How much are you depositing? I have to enter the amount,' she asked.

Ambika Devi took out the crumpled slip of paper on which Mariam had jotted down the total amount. She handed it to Tapasi, emphasizing each word: 'Fifty Thousand Eight Hundred and Thirty.' The man behind the counter wrote the amount on the slip and the form and counted the wad of currency notes Ambika Devi had amassed. Tapasi had never seen so much money in her life. She knew the treasure comprised of the cash donated to the ashram by philanthropists and the money raised by selling goods that had been given for the inmates. The money, which Ambika Devi was so brazenly putting into her personal account, rightfully belonged to all the inmates of the ashram.

The accountant returned Ambika Devi's passbook and remarked with a laugh, 'Your bank balance has really gone up, Behenji. Looks like you are earning a lot of money these days.'

'Yes, yes. I have rented out my house, you see. I have not been able to come here for several months,' she said quickly, and avoiding Tapasi's eye, put the passbook carefully back into her bag. Then she said, 'Let us go, Tapasi. Our work is done.'

Tapasi followed her outside. She noticed that the man

on the hillock was still standing there and lecturing fearlessly. His voice carried to where she stood:

'Do you know what place this is? This is Dwadashaditya Tila where Lord Krishna displayed his enormous strength and vanquished and killed massive demons! Great leaders of our country have stood here to address the masses and make false promises. This hillock is now a symbol of our shattered dreams and no one lights a lamp on the ruins over which the sun and rain beat relentlessly. Don't you think we too are sinking gradually into the ruins of ourselves?'

Just then a few people pushed through the crowd and lunged at the speaker. Grabbing him by the shoulders, they began to thrash him but he did not let up.

'These are hired goondas, pimps, impotent men, who have sold their souls! They can't bear the truth! Who is there to listen to the truth? Truth always gets thrashed when the administration is in the hands of hypocrites and dishonest people. Go on, brothers, beat me up! I'll still speak the truth because truth is not afraid! Go ahead, beat me because you get paid for it! What else do you know?' he shouted.

He braved the thrashing by steeling himself to the relentless punches, kicks and blows. A few people rushed to protect him but the crowd was more inclined towards violence at the time. Tapasi and Ambika Devi moved away from them. They managed to find a rickshaw only after walking a long distance. The clothes of the speaker were ripped now and blood trickled down his bare shoulders. He had fallen to the ground. Though he was silent his eyes were still eloquent. A couple of people picked him up and dumped him on the sidewalk—as if he wasn't a human being but a bag of stinking garbage. An old beggarwoman began to tend to his wounds and poured some water from her small earthen pitcher into his mouth. Tapasi couldn't tell whether he was conscious. The rickshaw moved on.

As they approached the next intersection, a woman with a man's face came and stood by them. She had long hair, kohl-lined eyes and a gold nose ring. She wore a gaudy red sari and a garland of flowers encircled her neck. She began singing a bhajan in the most tuneless fashion. When she opened her mouth to sing, four broken teeth added to her repulsive appearance. Tapasi felt nauseated. She got off the rickshaw and began to throw up violently in the drain beside the footpath.

'Hey, what's happened to you? Are you all right?' Ambika Devi exclaimed as she helped Tapasi onto the rickshaw again. She was annoyed with her but could not chide her because of the crowd that had assembled around them. 'I didn't know you were so soft—you get upset over such trifling things. These things happen here everyday. It is just a show. *Saale*, they are social workers in name only. No real work is done by them. They just provoke innocent people and publish nonsensical things in the newspapers. That man is utterly shameless. He gets beaten everytime but he rises up again. He comes to this spot and speaks over and over. He is out of his mind.'

Suddenly, the rickshaw lurched and the woman with the man's face was right in front of them. She put out her palms to beg and Tapasi noticed that there were *swastika* marks on her hand. Ambika Devi addressed her angrily, 'How dare you come here? You wretched hijra, don't you have anything better to do than beg?'

'You called me a hijra, did you?' Devdasi answered in a thunderous voice, 'I am not a beggar. I am a devdasi. I perform puja. I'm living a curse. And don't I know you? So arrogant about being a woman! Leaving your husband to live with another! Just look at your face! Pretending to be a *sati savitri!* A cat who goes on pilgrimage after devouring a hundred mice! *Saali Behenji*...getting fatter and fatter on the unlawful gains at the widows' ashram!' The woman had started frothing at the mouth. Tapasi felt sick again. The rickshaw-puller tried to pedal faster. Ambika Devi's face had turned ashen. Loud words of abuse and derision followed them. 'You run a prostitution racket. Who does not know that your ashram is a brothel! *Saali*...you call one who worships God a hijra?'

'She is crazy. Don't pay attention to what she says, okay? And listen don't say anything about all this,' Ambika Devi instructed Tapasi.

As soon as they reached the ashram, Tapasi jumped off the rickshaw, rushed to the water tap and threw up. Relieved, she sipped some water and wrapped the wet pallu of her sari around her forehead. Then she applied herself to her work. If she did not do so, she would be deprived of her two rotis of the day.

Tapasi curled up under her new blanket at night but sleep eluded her. The eyes of the man who had been beaten up haunted her. There was something about them that made her restless. How could she define that something? A kind of detachment had glimmered through those eyes as he'd continued to speak despite being thrashed. What was behind the resolute expression suspended like a dark cloud in those eyes? Was it the truth of that man—his integrity—that showed through his resolute detachment under such stress? Did that mean that truth was so powerful it could keep a man calmly dispassionate even when he was being tortured? She remembered what Mariam had told her once, 'Each one of us possesses the truth, Tapasi. We all know about truth but it is extremely difficult to survive with total commitment to truth.'

IT WAS TAKING them a long time to reach Goverdhan. They had started much before dawn. The sun had not come up yet and the morning breeze was moist and pleasantly cool. The women were cheerful and uninhibited as Ambika Devi was not chaperoning them. They had ventured out on an unfamiliar path, away from their restricted life. Though they had some vague images of it in their mind they did not know what Goverdhan would actually be like. A road, partially metalled and partially dirt, stretched out before them and their minds were full of eager curiosity. What would Goverdhan be like? It was the fabled playground of Kanha, the lover God, and he came here to graze his cows and disport with the milkmaids of Braj, filling the whole place with colour and melody. It was said that all six seasons existed here simultaneously. The very rocks of the hills were exotic. They had shapes and colours different from other rocks. The caves, waterfalls and bowers around had all borne witness to their Kanhai's intimate and public dalliances. It was believed that the place was still aglow with the lingering warmth of Sri Krishna and Radhika's bodies. The priest at the temple had told them that mere contact with the mountain absolved all sins committed in all births.

The sun was rising now. Tapasi noticed the air grow

vibrant with a golden-red glow, as if some invisible being was beckoning her, speaking to her. She wondered if this pilgrimage and the spiritual merit earned through it would open a new chapter in her life. She offered prayers with true faith for the first time—to the sun, to the invisible sacred mountain, Giriraj, or maybe to the dawn of a new possibility. Noorabai, who did not even know what her religion was, walked with her. She knew no Gods or Goddesses. Her problem was as basic as the fire in her belly and any food that made itself available was the object of her worship. Then there was Barota. Harsh, brazen, Barota who only understood her sexual urges and needs. God and religion were a farce for her. Mariam had been born a Christian but she lived in the land of Krishna as if it was her home. As for Vrinda, her faith and her religion began and ended with poor, crippled Chuniya. She was completely committed to seeing her daughter well. How infinite her patience was. How single-minded.

The poor souls. Tired, defeated minds struggling with pain—gathered under one roof, where they could hold each other's hands when the misery grew unbearable. What had their religion saddled them with anyway, other than an oppressive seriousness and an anxiety of the future? They were friends because of their unnatural circumstances, and helped and supported each other because friendship has a special vision—making it able to see things which are not immediately apparent.

As they walked, they came upon an entrancing water reservoir to the right of the road, presided over by an elaborately carved sandstone edifice. There were four turrets on the four corners of the building, and a winding staircase that led to impressive platforms which formed the viewers' galleries. The scummy green water in the pond rippled playfully. The name of the place was engraved on a marble slab outside: 'Kusum Sarovar'—Lake of Flowers.

Tapasi was delighted. She imagined a place full of flowers. So far, all she had seen were narrow streets and bazaars with piles of trash. She ran ahead of the others and began to climb down the steps to the pond.

'Where does the water come from and where does it go? There is no river here,' Bhagwati queried.

'Who knows,' said Barota. 'But how does it concern you where the water comes from? Come on, keep moving. If we go on stopping like this we won't be able to perform the *parikrama*.' Barota urged them forward and they began to follow her like rivers that move towards the ocean. But Tapasi's mind held a big question. She wanted to know who had built the Kusum Sarovar and to what end. She did not want to go on without taking a good look at the pond.

'Let us go and see the temple at least, Barota. We'll go up for a while,' said Tapasi and without waiting for a reply, took Mariam's hand and ran up the stairs, reaching a spacious terrace in the centre of which was a dome-shaped structure that looked like a temple. An old man sat at the open door of the structure bent over a book from which he read in soft murmurs. Tapasi was struck by the thought that this was probably the first time she had seen a priest reading a book since she had come to these parts. All the others were either praying or conducting business in the name of worship.

The man noticed Tapasi and shouted, 'Where are you going? What do you want?'

'We want to go for darshan,' answered Tapasi. By now, Noorabai and Barota had entered the shrine. It was a neat little temple. A small marble tablet with the imprint of two feet was placed in the centre.

"Whose feet are these, Baba?' Tapasi could not help asking.

'These are the imprints of the Lord's feet,' he replied, and adjusting the string with which his broken spectacles were looped around his ear, took a good look at all the women.

'And this pond?' Vrinda asked a question for once.

'It is called Kusum Sarovar, *beti*. Legend has it that there was once a forest full of white flowers here. Once, when Radha Rani came here to gather flowers for puja, she looked around for a spring where she could wash the flowers she had gathered but she found none. The Lord sensed her dilemma in a moment and created this pond by digging the earth with his flute. Since then this pond has always remained full. The water here never dries. Moreover, this place is sacred because Sri Krishna sat by this very pond and combed Radha Rani's hair with his fingers. Look, there is a picture depicting that scene on the wall.'

Tapasi looked at the mural which depicted, in time-worn colours, Radha with long hair and Lord Krishna wearing a crown of peacock feathers. The two were painted in an extremely soulful attitude. Tapasi felt a stirring in her heart, a new and unfamiliar sensation she had not experienced before. 'Tell me more about this place, please,' she begged the old man.

'But how impatient you are! Well, this temple was built by Raja Surajmal of Bharatpur four hundred years ago. I've been the pandit of this place since 1936. I've never been away from here. I reside here, at the sacred feet of the Lord. My frugal needs are met by the benevolence of Braj Bihariji. I was born on this soil, *beti*, and I wish to be immersed here after I die.' Baba stood up leaning on his stick. Driven by some impulse, Tapasi began to follow him. After walking some distance, Baba stopped at a blue zinc-plated door. Baba offered them *charnamrit* and explained, 'This is the temple of Uddhavji. This temple was built five thousand years ago by Lord Krishna's grandson. There are only three abodes of Uddhavji—Dwarka, Badrikashram and here. Uddhavji, Krishna's closest friend, is all over this place, manifesting himself in the form of groves and creepers, in the hope of being touched by the feet of the Lord or Radha Rani and obtaining deliverance.'

'Does that mean he has not yet obtained deliverance, Baba? Even after so much love and devotion?'

Barota tried to restrain Tapasi. 'Tapasi, you get absorbed in conversation wherever you go. You ask strange questions. Come, get up and get going. If we keep stopping like this, when will we do *parikrama*?'

'You are right.' Tapasi was about to stand up when she noticed a woman offering yellow flowers to the idol of Uddhavji. Baba gave her *charnamrit* and asked. 'How are you Gauur Dasi? The world may go topsy-turvy but your routine will not change. Are you going for *parikrama* today?'

'Yes I am, Baba. I was delayed today because my cow has fallen sick. I tended her all night. I have managed to come out only now. I find no peace till I have done darshan of Giriraj.'

Pandit Baba nodded and began to recite a couplet:

Adiloke baikunth mem braj paripooran soye
Brajwasi hitkarne aayo hari giri hoye.

For the first time in her life Tapasi wished to make an offering at a temple. She had not brought any flowers with her but she did have some money tied to the pallu of her sari. She took out a rupee and placed it on the palm of Pandit Baba. She was suddenly reminded of a poem she had read in a magazine in Bolepur.

Bhookh se ririyati hui phaili hatheli ka naam daya hai
Aur bhookh se tani muthhi ka nam
Naxalbari hai.

But before she could begin to reminisce about her forgotten Bolepur and the Naxalbari movement spreading through Bengal, Noorabai grabbed her by the arm and said, 'Will you get a move on now? Barota is hopping mad. Besides, there is that ascetic woman who is on her way to *parikrama*. If we go along with her we won't lose our way. Come now.'

'All right.' Tapasi began walking with them. On seeing her, Barota said, 'How many places are you going to stop at, Tapasi? Kusum Sarovar is not the only lake here. You'll come across Radha Kund, Lalita Kund and Narad Kund and many others strewn all over the place.'

'Really?' Tapasi exclaimed and then wide-eyed, started searching for other places like Kusum Sarovar. Barota struck up a conversation with Gauur Dasi who told her that she was a native of Khulna, now in Bangladesh. Mujibur Rehman, the Bangladeshi President, had also been from the same town. She belonged to a family that was so poor that the three women in it had just one sari amongst them, which they wore by turns. Her poverty and hunger had tossed her from man to man. She was bought and sold, caught and released, many times before she'd been able to reach this place. She stayed for long in an ashram in Goverdhan where the woman in charge, Ma Chandrika, was a truly remarkable woman. Ma Chandrika kept a silver idol of baby Krishna, Balagopal, in her room. The idol was offered bhog at 4 am everyday. Most of the inmates and visitors to the ashram were foreign women. Ma Chandrika spoke English with them. On one occasion, a foreigner had brought a bag of imported potato wafers with her which she left on Ma Chandrika's table. The ashram prohibited the use of foreign goods but they all saw potato wafer crumbs sticking to the Balagopal's mouth and the crumpled packet lying next to the idol. It had been an extraordinary experience for all of them.

'Which ashram do you stay in now?' Mariam asked.

'None...I got a raw deal in all the ashrams. I spent time in several of them. In one ashram at Mathura, the flesh trade was carried out openly. I too was forced into it. The members of the managing committee there were not decent people. They treated us like dogs, robbed and cheated us. A few of the women dared to report the matter to the police, but are the police human beings? Their lechery was more unbearable. Who would listen to our complaints? Our biggest offence was that we were women and that we were young. We escaped their advances at night but had to pay for it during the day. One of the women who was with us died of starvation. Now I work for a family as their domestic help. They've given me a room at the back of their house. They pay me enough to keep me going. One day, a sickly stray cow stopped by my room and I've been taking care of her ever since.'

'Is that why you are called Gauur Dasi?'

'Yes, I do not have any other anchor or base. The cow is everything to me—mother, sister, everything.' Her eyes glowed with quiet contentment.

They walked for a long time, through the bazaars, on slushy dirt tracks and unpaved pathways, inspired by Gauur Dasi's fervour but the mountain was nowhere in sight. All they saw were hordes of old, ailing women, and handicapped men and children, out to beg. Like Giriraj Goverdhan caving into the earth, the phenomenon of a collapsed administration made Tapasi's heart sink. Tapasi and her companions moved along with the other pilgrims who stopped to drink the sherbet and grab the prasad which was being distributed free by other faithfuls on the road. The crowd also had devotees who were performing the *parikrama* the hard way—by rolling on the ground. Everyone pressed on as single-mindedly as if walking was their only purpose. It was as if they were walking to salvation. No one complained of the pain caused by the gravel and shingles underfoot. They went past several ponds and pools of water, all with stories attached to them—old, crumbling *havelis* and ruined temples rife with heady stories of Lord Krishna's amorous dalliances, which the moving crowd excitedly commented upon.

Tapasi was lost in her thoughts. She felt as though someone was whispering into her ear but she couldn't understand what he was saying. Presently they came to a small pond surrounded by a crumbling boundary wall. Gauur Dasi told them, 'This is the spot where Lord Krishna sat and enjoyed his afternoon meal with cowherds and milkmaids. This pond is called Gover Pokhar.'

Soon the city and the bazaar were left far behind and they were approaching Giriraj Goverdhan. There were no woods, nor any flowers. Only a few rocks and the stump of a blunted hillock to suggest that tall mountain peaks might have existed there in the past. The women began to touch the rocks as if that contact itself would bring about their deliverance. Tapasi touched them too. She admitted to herself that the rocks did emit a subtle vibration and even a light contact with them touched one deep within. As they came closer, the rocky hillock seemed to grow a little taller. They climbed it quickly and thought themselves lucky to have to climb only a small mountain. They wanted to sit and relax for a while but their attention was diverted by the presence of a small, half-submerged cave nearby and they entered it one by one.

The cave was not only narrow but enclosed on all sides. There was no passage for fresh air. Tapasi noticed a person sitting in the cave with a small oil lamp in front of him. Feeling suffocated, most of the others beat a hasty retreat but Tapasi was curious, so she moved in further. She heard Gauur Dasi say, 'A Baba resides in this cave. He never steps out of here. Wonder how he keeps alive. One can't even breathe properly in here.'

Just then, the stifled air of the cave reverberated with the Baba's booming voice: 'Om, Om.' His voice seemed to cleanse the whole expanse of the cave right up to the top. Each time 'Om' echoed off the walls of the cave, it cleansed the air all over again. The sound of Baba's voice seemed to transform into a gust of fresh air each time he pronounced the word. It was a most intriguing phenomenon. Tapasi wondered what it was that kept Baba from suffocating. Was it the Lord's name, the power in his own voice, or something else?

◆◆◆

They all came out of the cave and proceeded further. Gauur Dasi was their guide. She pointed out the sights. 'This is Jugal Kund, this is Killol Kund and this one is Paanch Teertha Ganga. Come now, look, that is Maanasi Ganga over there. Let's take a dip in it then move on.'

'No, no. We don't want to bathe. We'll be delayed,' Bhagwati protested looking at Barota.

'Now that you've stepped out of the ashram today, you should make the most of every opportunity. A bath in

Maanasi Ganga is as sacred an act as bathing in Bhagirathi Ganga. Not only does it wash off your sins but it also awakens the love of God in your heart. Moreover, this river is shrinking like Giriraj and will disappear someday,' Gauur Dasi said.

'You are calling it Ganga. But how can the Ganga be here?'

'I'll answer you in a moment. Come and see the lake where Sri Krishna first went boating with Sri Radhaji.'

There were many people standing by the edge of the pool, some with their eyes closed, others reciting slokas and still others taking dips in the water. Vrinda and Bhagwati took off their saris and waded into the water. Mariam sat down on the steps. Tapasi moved close to Gauur Dasi and scooping some water in her hands, sprinkled it on her body.

'You haven't told me about Maanasi Ganga,' she said.

Gauur Dasi looked at her. 'You sound educated. What is your name?'

'Tapasi.'

'You aren't like the other widows. How come you are here?'

'It is my destiny. I studied up to class twelve. Now, since circumstances have brought me here, I'd like to know all about this city and this teertha. I want to understand its mystique and how it became a place of pilgrimage.'

'Do you teach in a school?'

'No, I don't. I understand a little Hindi but I know

Bengali and English,' Tapasi said diffidently.

'English teachers earn more money. There is an English school here, Tapasi. You should look for a job there. You have a long life ahead of you. Don't throw it away. I'll let you know if there are any openings for you. I'll ask the people in whose house I work.'

A silence fell between the two. After a while, Gauur Dasi spoke again, 'Okay, now I'll tell you about Maanasi Ganga. On one occasion Krishna and Balaram were out grazing the cows when a demon named Vrishbhasur disguised himself as a cow and joined the herd. Lord Krishna, being omniscient, recognized him at once and going straight up to him, grabbed him by his hind legs and whirled him round and round before flinging him up into the sky. The demon crashed back to earth and just before he died, he reverted from a cow to his real self. However, a cow murder is a murder, so the herdsmen charged the Lord with killing a cow and exhorted him to bathe in the Ganga, otherwise he would not be absolved of his sin. The Lord did penance to bring Ganga to Braj and Ganga gushed right out of his heart and entered this pool! Maanas means heart. That is why this place is recognized as Maanasi Kund.'

'You are so knowledgeable, Gauur Dasi! Are you educated too?'

'No. But I have given myself to Vrindavan. I tell you, I've lived such a terrible life. There is no hardship I've not borne.

No suffering has spared me. And now there is the loneliness. But I am sheltered at the feet of the Lord. My cow is my centre of pilgrimage. I'm committed to her service. That is all.'

Vrinda was back from her dip. 'We may as well go and perform puja in the temple of Maanasi Devi,' she suggested, so they entered the temple. Gauur Dasi said, 'Maharaj, could you please perform a *gul gul* puja for us?'

'O you Bengali women! You have left your desh behind but have not forgotten *gul gul* puja! Okay, make your offering. Have you brought some fruit and flowers or are you empty-handed?'

'A poor widow's hands always remain empty, Baba. If you could conduct a puja for us, we'd be grateful.'

Instead of reciting the mantras to commence the puja the priest began to abuse the women, all the while winding the three idols with skeins of red thread over and over again. These babas, pandits and pujaris, sitting by the idols of God in every temple, are as brazen as beggars, thought Tapasi. There is no humility in their conduct. They demand money as if it is their right. So what if their clothes and appearance are different. They beg for goods and money in the name of offerings to the idols.

Gauur Dasi produced a five-rupee note from her blouse and looked at Baba with moist eyes that glimmered victoriously. Even a beggar like Gauur Dasi immediately started behaving like a master when she gave.

The *gul gul* puja commenced. After the priest recited the extra mantras all the women closed their eyes. This was followed by ululations and chants of the words *gul gul* as they bowed over and over. Tapasi found the whole process ridiculous. She wanted to laugh but she could not. Maybe because she had forgotten how. She had no wish to offend anybody so she sat quietly with folded hands. If Ganga had come to this region, so had Bengal. And these poor Bengali wretches had come here and spread like poisoned blood in a diseased body.

◆◆◆

They were on the last leg of their *padyatra* and had reached the final rock of Goverdhan called the Mukharwind Shila, where a large number of devotees had congregated. Tapasi and her group watched curiously as a priest smeared vermilion on a round black stone and wound a red string around it. Then, chanting mantras, he poured a bucketful of milk over it—as casually as if it was water! He poured many more bucketfuls. The faces of the women blanched as they watched the process. Finally, Noora could not take it any more. She burst into tears and lamented, 'My poor children were deprived of milk. They had to be sold. My husband starved to death. But look at you, *saala* You are pouring this milk like water and wasting it!'

Her words startled the faithful who stared at Noora who was like one possessed. She waved her arms in the air, let out a torrent of expletives, and screamed at the top of her voice, 'We don't even get to see milk. There are so many poor women like us who have not tasted milk in years and hypocrites like you are pouring it down the drain in the name of God. Do stones ever drink milk? Don't you have any sense? Aren't you ashamed of yourselves?' She would have slapped the priest had Barota not stepped forward and restrained her. They were all a little unnerved by their friend's outburst. The pujari and the others around him had found an excuse to abuse them.

'Who are these bloody bitches? This witch has contaminated the puja. You'll have to suffer the wrath of Srinathji. Throw her out, the wretch! Lord knows where all these whores come from...and land up here to die!'

Someone hurled a stone at Noora. Weak with hunger and thirst as she was, she keeled over and fell down. The blood trickling out of her head mixed with the milk as it slopped into the drain. It was a peculiar sight. Milk, flowing to the chant of mantras, and the blood of an impure, low-caste widow, merging with one another and flowing as one into the gutter.

Vrinda laughed hollowly, '*Saale*, who do you think made us whores? You asshole... people like you. Call yourself a pandit because you wear a tikka on your forehead? You are naked under your yellow robes too.'

MADAN MOHAN BABA had cast away his mortal frame and all of Vrindavan seemed to have congregated to mourn his passing. You could hear the sound of bhajans being sung to the accompaniment of drums and cymbals and mantras. Tapasi watched with astonishment as preparations got underway to place Baba's body in a state of *samadhi* on a float. The float was to be taken all over town.

The procession started. Four men carried the float on their shoulders. Baba's body was propped up into a sitting position and supported by an iron rod. From a distance the body did not look like a corpse. More like an impressive sanyasi sitting in meditation. The air was heavy with the chanting of Baba's name and eulogies sung in his praise.

The procession returned to the muth in the evening. The wooden divan on which Baba used to sit was put in his room and his body placed on it. A day went by, then another, but nobody performed the last rites. The disciples at the muth were from Harinam Sampradaya and professed a deep faith in Sri Krishna. The founder-in-chief of the sect decided that the Baba should not be cremated because then he would return and re-enter the same body to start a new life. The other priests and sadhus of the city tried to reason with the chief but to no avail.

A basement of sorts was rigged up in the space of four days and was fashioned into a resting place for Baba. A bed was set in the middle and his body placed on it in an attitude of *samadhi*. Perfumed oils, herbal pastes and chemical substances were applied to preserve the body. The place was sealed and made completely airtight with strong masonry work. Senior police officials visited the muth and much political pressure was exercised to prevent this strange burial but the muth officials refused to listen to anyone. Religion was the most important thing here. Everything else was immaterial! The controversy over Baba's last rites raged for a few days. A few articles appeared in the newspapers but the authorities at the muth refused to budge. Once, a couple of people dislodged a brick of the basement to catch a glimpse of the Baba but they were hit by a blast of stench so violent that, subsequently, no one else dared do any such thing. Meanwhile, Baba's disciples continued to claim they could hear the sound of Baba's footsteps and the sound of him doing jaap at night.

No one knew what to believe—whether Baba was in *samadhi* or not. But for Tapasi, it was a most astonishing event. For days, she was not able to forget Baba's dead body, the attitude of meditation in which he sat and the procession with the float. Thinking about it at night she would get scared. At times she felt the presence of someone in wooden sandals standing beside her. A gust, a stench, would leave her feeling sick and restless. She wondered if Baba was really meditating in a *samadhi* and whether he would really come back. The fact that he was a hundred and ten years old was proof in itself that he was no ordinary mortal. The founder of the muth was heard saying that when the energy, effected by Baba's meditation, flowed towards Baba's pulse, it would resume its beat and he would begin to breathe again. He would then return in exactly the same form that he had been before.

◆◆◆

A great feast was organized on the day of Baba's *shraadh* and all the inmates of the Sri Radha Krishna Vidhwa Ashram partook of the feast, sitting cross-legged on the floor, amongst the rows of guests. Vrinda wheedled the officials of the muth for some food for her daughter and returned with a basket laden with food. This was during the rains and poor Chuniya, who was so used to hunger, gorged on cucumber, watermelon and stale, sticky sweets. Consequently, she got severe gastro-enteritis. She threw up all day and all night. Vrinda's room stank to high heaven. Food, which was meant to nourish the body, turned to poison and septicemia set in. The frail Vrinda staggered out of her room carrying her unconscious child in her arms. She wailed, 'Chuniya has fallen unconscious. Look, she does not even open her eyes. She is not even crying. Please call a doctor, Behenji. Please help.'

Barota happened to be passing by with a bucket full of water. She poured the water on Chuniya saying, 'There is vomit all over her. Who is going to touch her?'

But life, like a little bird, had already flown away from little Chuniya's emaciated body.

Bhagwati said, 'Whoever calls a doctor to the ashram? You must be mad, Vrinda.'

Noorabai touched Chuniya's hand. 'She is not alive, Vrinda. Your child is dead.' Then she broke into peals of laughter. 'Your daughter has died, Vrinda. My children have been pawned away too. My Nanda... Oh where is my Nanda?' And then she began to cry. Her crying was like the lava gushing out of a volcano, a raging fire of lament.

'O my poor Chuniya has died so young. What had she seen of life? What comfort have I in the world? She has gone leaving me forlorn. She was my only anchor. What'll I do now.. .whom will I look after? O my Chuniya!'

Bhagwati said, 'What could Chuniya have seen of life? With those crippled legs of hers what world would she have gone to? Yours and mine. What had this world offered her, anyway?'

'You should thank *Radhey maiya* that your lame girl has gone! What would she do even if she'd lived? She would have begged in the streets or slept with the beggars. What other future did she have, tell me? Good that she got her deliverance!' Barota spat on Chuniya's body.

Vrinda glared at her with bloodshot eyes. 'You would know if you had given birth. You base woman, how dare you spit on my daughter's body? The vile things you indulge in... leprosy will claim you one day... God does not spare anyone.'

Barota grabbed Vrinda's neck and yelled, 'I'll tell you who indulges in vile things and who'll get the disease. You are the one who is afflicted with leprosy!'

Vrinda's body went limp in Barota's vice-like grip. Tapasi urged her over and over again to release Vrinda but when Barota ignored her pleas, she struck her across the face with a resounding slap. Reeling under its impact, Barota let go of Vrinda. All the others stood and watched in stunned silence.

'You slapped me, Tapasi! How dare you?' Barota growled but by that time Ambika Devi had arrived in the courtyard of the ashram. She covered her nose and surveyed the scene, chiding the women.

'Is there any difference between you and animals? What is all this ruckus about? What a mess this place is! Go, get a bucket of water and clean up this place. Why do you fight all the time? Come on, Vrinda, take the child out of here. I'll just send for the *doms*. They'll come and take her away.'

'Please, Behenji, don't send for the *doms*. I'll carry her in my arms. She was the daughter of a Brahmin. I'll immerse her body in Gangaji. My poor child got nothing out of life.' Vrinda's tears, the tears of a bereaved mother, just would not stop.

Tapasi remembered someone telling her that the water of the Ganga was so holy and pure that it never got polluted and the miraculous thing was that the bones of the dead just dissolved in it. The Ganga absorbed the deceased so completely that not an atom of their body remained in it. All the five elements of the body were subsumed in the original elements from which they had been constituted.

'She is out of her mind,' Ambika Devi thundered. 'She wants the water of Ganga for her lame girl. And just look at her gumption...She is referring to the girl as a Brahmin's child! So, why don't you call that bastard of a father here? Let him come and give a proper funeral to this proof of his sins!'

'She is not the only one. Even the others have become bold here,' said Barota looking at Tapasi menacingly. Ambika Devi and Barota laughed. No one else joined in. Their malicious laughter ricocheted off the dusty walls of the ashram and reverberated in the silence of death.

Shortly thereafter, two ugly, black-skinned men entered the ashram. They wore only dhotis. Thin sacred threads ran across their hairy chests. Vrinda began to tremble with fear. The men's faces were so pitiless that the very air seemed to rustle with terror in their presence. They snatched little Chuniya from the arms of a screaming Vrinda, wrapped her in a length of dirty cloth, and vanished into the darkness of the night.

Overcome by the cruelty of the whole scene, Tapasi asked, 'What will they do to Chuniya, Behenji? Will they cremate her?' She remembered Majumdar Babu's funeral pyre.

'Are you crazy? Small children are not cremated. They are buried under a slab and soil. Animals then devour them. Okay now, Tapasi. You have become too talkative. Come on everybody, go and get water and clean up the room and the courtyard. How awful the place smells!'

Ambika Devi's orders and her harsh face were enough to propel them into action. They got up and went to fetch water.

The routine of the ashram was resumed as if nothing had happened. Chuniya's whimpers, her poor health and pitiable death belonged to another day. Vrinda still cried. Tapasi's wounded pigeon had responded to just a little love, a little care, and recovered. Chuniya had been a human being. Vrinda was a human being too. Big deal.

◆◆◆

Tapasi had had no exposure to death in her childhood but now, having spent two years in the ashram, she recognized it fully. Of late, she had become acutely aware of how her circumstances had increased her vulnerability and defencelessness. She had begun to realize that the confusion she was experiencing was caused by one central problem. The problem was the conflict between what she ought to have been and what she had become. She agonized over the question relating to her present life and wondered how long she could go on this way.

Everytime Tapasi sat down and sang bhajans in front of the idols, the fixed smile of the Lord filled her with seething resentment. His smile seemed to mock at her situation. The chiming of the temple bells created a storm inside her shaking her very existence. 'What brings you here? Why do you come and sit here?' The very air inside the sanctum sanctorum of the temple seemed to jeer.

Tapasi had coped with these disturbing feelings for a long time but now she realized she could not take it any more. The contradictions within her were making her go to piccces. Lying quietly in her room at night she felt the darkness writing exclusive messages for her on the wall. But she did not know what the messages said. What she knew was that the intense gloom of the room was not going to be dispelled by the faint light of the bulb in the veranda. Feeble hands do not bring about a change. It was imperative to make her hands as strong as rocks. A lot had been written in her blue notebook by now. She was going to buy a new notebook soon. The pile of newspapers near her pillow grew steadily higher. She read every scrap of old newsprint so assiduously that she had slowly begun to comprehend them. The newspapers provided tantalizing glimpses of an external world and broadened her vision.

One day, walking towards the temple, Tapasi noticed that the number of visitors and beggars outside Baba's *samadhi* had swelled. Some of the beggars were genuinely old and handicapped while others had bandaged their hands and feet or sat feigning blindness to move onlookers to reach for their purses. How could one decide between the real and the fake? Her eyes fell on a man sitting among a row of beggars. The man was trying to hide his face with a torn sheet wrapped around his head and shoulders but the sheet kept slipping off his face. His posture suggested deep pain. As soon as the meal was served, he began to eat but with great difficulty. There was something about him that arrested Tapasi's attention and curiosity. Those eyes...there was something about them... Yes, he was the same person. The eyes and posture of people who stand and make fiery speeches acquire the power to mesmerize... It was the same man. She went up to him.

'What happened? You used to speak of such lofty things. Your speeches were full of the truth. How come you are reduced to this?'

The journalist opened his mouth with great effort. Tapasi was shocked to see that his tongue had been cut off. He stood up trembling with pain and humiliation. Before Tapasi could say another word, he got up and staggered off. She was stunned for a while then she burst into copious tears. Herself on the verge of tears, Noorabai pulled her away and took her to a crumbling parapet where they sat in silence for a long time.

'It's time for *aarti*,' Noorabai reminded her after a while. Tapasi wiped her tears. Her mind was in torment. The thinking of that man, his ability to tell the truth, the relevance of his words, the power of his speech...Did all that mean nothing? Was it impractical, senseless prattle? Does it mean that one should not speak? Is that why Mauni Baba was silent? The silence of Mauni Baba and that of the tongueless man who was punished for speaking out, were astounding.

In the days that followed, Tapasi felt as if there was a thorn in her being—a poisonous thorn that caused ceaseless torment. The more she thought about herself and all that she had witnessed, the sharper the thorn pricked. Her entire sensibility converged on that acutely sensitive centre of pain. She went about her routine at the temple and the ashram in a mechanical fashion. Her heart was not in anything. She was finding it increasingly difficult to sit before the idols in the temple. The frozen smiles on their faces taunted her. The sound of temple bells set off a storm in her mind. She realized that if she wanted to find a way out of this world of temples and idols, she would have to leap over them. There was bound to be a way out but who was there to show it to her?

◆◆◆

The Lord seems to have a broader smile on his face today, thought Tapasi, as she entered the temple that day. What is he smiling at? Is he smiling at the new girl cowering by Barota's side or the inflammation and pain in Noorabai's infected eyes? Is the Lord just a stone smiling at the pain of others—an inanimate object—an object without a heart, who does not understand the language nor wishes to. And if it is so, what is the relevance of all these bhajans and jaaps? Are they just a worthless cacophony of hollow sounds with no meaning? The tongue of one who utters meaningful phrases is cut off mercilessly and the Lord allows it.

As on other days, the slimy looking pujari mechanically dressed the stone idols. He bathed them in a concoction of ghee, honey, Gangajal and milk. Then they were draped in silk clothes, adorned with silver, gold and floral ornaments and anointed with perfume. The bhog, consisting of fruit and an array of sweets, was readied. Tapasi watched the rituals dully. They had not eaten a morsel since morning. The feeling of gnawing hunger was a permanent state with them. The new saris that had been donated to the ashram had been sold by Ambika Devi two days ago. Her bank balance was swelling. The Lord was happy. That is why he smiled from his richly decorated pavilion. Tapasi wondered why the Lord was being readied. Was it for a new onslaught of bitterness, pain and disaster? Clenched firmly in Barota's grip, the new girl at the ashram was crying bitterly. The *keertan* was in progress

—cymbals, dholaks and the thumping rhythmic chant of *Radhey Shyam*, to the accompaniment of the tears of the sad new eyes. The nectar of piety flowed freely, mingling with the ghee dripping from the hands of the pujari. Everything seemed to melt and merge as Tapasi moved away from her centre. The distance grew steadily. There were so many faces, so many tears shed and unshed, drowning in the noises that seemed to deafen her. A thundering cacophony rocked her being, leading now to dizziness, now to nausea. She knew she could not take it any more. Violating the regulations of the temple, she got up from her appointed place and the cymbals clattered onto the marble floor as they slipped out of her hands—the sound they made like an announcement heralding her flight. Tapasi was screaming. The bhajan stopped. The new girl in Barota's clutches extricated herself and began shouting, 'Let go of me, let go of me!' The pujari, the crowd of believers, and the bhajan singing widows, all stared at Tapasi in bewilderment. They were stunned by the arbitrary screams that were so much at variance with meditation, devotion and worship—the general constituents of temple life.

Tapasi ran out through the door, totally oblivious to her existence, or non-existence. She felt light and transparent, like air, formless as a river without banks and yet engulfed by an endless stretch of old memories that surrounded her like a sky covered with black smoke. She ran out and stood on the open platform outside the temple screaming hysterically, 'I can't do it! I can't stand it anymore!' The new girl had come running after her but instead of crying she stood transfixed, in a state where the body petrifies and tears dry out.

Suddenly, the pigeon Tapasi had brought back from the brink of death, made an appearance and perched on a turret of the temple, cooing softly. Tapasi noticed him through her tears. All at once she had a vision of a bridge suspended from the wings of the pigeon which would take her to the land of her dreams. There was joy in that fragile faith but joy and fear signified the same end as far as she was concerned. She knew she could not bank on joy, and fear would reclaim her soon. But she would make an effort. No matter what, she would not allow her tree of courage to be uprooted. She would leap and follow the path of light the pigeon had showed her. But where was it—this path of light?

◆◆◆

How she survived the next two days, she didn't know. All she remembered were Barota's dark face with its incongruous brown eyes—and her cane—wielding, tyrannical hands. She was beaten blue and black. The bloodstains on her sari had dried and blackened. She hadn't eaten in two days and she was on the verge of collapse when Mariam sneaked in from what seemed to be a secret door and held a cracked plastic mug full of milk to her mouth, 'Come, drink it, otherwise you'll die.'

The other door was open. Someone shouted , 'Let her die. How does it matter to us?'

'Indeed, I should die.' Tapasi thought, 'I should really die. Death would be better than this life of purposeless breathing and this broken, beaten body. What is left in the wreck that I am anyway' At the same moment her mind was seized with another feeling—an intense longing to see her bullock-cart and the Chhatim tree in Vishwa Bharti. It was an extraordinary feeling.

When she surfaced again she saw a fire burning in a hearth. Noorabai was applying dry, hot fomentation to her body with a pestle heated in the hearth. 'Has the pain lessened somewhat?' she asked sympathetically.

Tapasi made no answer. Vrinda sighed her own bereavement, 'Does the pain ever get less?'

Tapasi did not have the strength to speak but her mind was racing. She thought, Fire is a strange thing. It cooks the food that nourishes our body on the one hand and burns and reduces it to ashes on the other. The warmth of the fire in the hearth brought her comfort in her pain but another raged uncontrollably within her. She was not going to put up with her situation any more. Countless blows of Ambika Devi's cane, pain and hunger, all had been borne without complaint. Barota had subjected her to her own brand of tyranny inside a closed room. Mariam and Noorabai reasoned with her but she was determined.

Part II

IT WAS A small settlement, undistinguished by the presence of a river, a mountain or a historical ruin. Still, it was a colony of sorts located somewhere in the heart of Bolepur town. With just a scatter of houses, some of unbaked brick, the place could hardly be called a village, let alone pass as an 'urban' area. It could have been named anything like 'Belgharia', 'Naihati' or 'Kanchanpara' but the name on the signboard of the municipal park was blurred and faded—quite impossible to read—and the settlement was nameless. Subjected to the city's contempt, the park was nothing more than a patch of wild grass with a couple of big and small trees. If no roses had ever bloomed here, then neither, frankly, had any mushrooms and moulds. Across the park was a road shaded by Chhahel trees that led to an old mohalla which had been transformed into an impressive residential complex. It was impressive because of its distinguished intellectual residents—the teachers of Vishwa Bharti. Tapasi lived in a house in the nameless basti across the park. It was not clear what her being there meant—whether her life was just drifting along or whether there was a direction to it. The house consisted of a partially covered veranda and a courtyard with a shady banyan tree. It had two residents—a very young Tapasi and Rakhal, whom she called Kaka. Even at that tender age, Tapasi was given to contemplation. Her child mind was forever flooded with questions—curiosity, inquiry and astonishment were integral to her personality. Inquisitive by nature, she was attracted to everything and questions simply tumbled out of her mind. Kaka, whoever he was, she didn't really know, was her only help and her only protector. He fascinated and repelled her. Everytime she looked at the stumpy man and his twisted ugly face she wondered how he sculpted such exquisite statues. When he raised his chisel and struck rock with it, it was as if a divine power wafted into the stone. Watching the beautiful figure slowly emerge from under the chisel in his hand, Tapasi felt the sculpture come alive, felt the misshapen rock breathe and turn into something ethereal. The experience of watching such creativity at work became integral to Tapasi's sensibility, both real and fantastic.

◆◆◆

Life in that small house followed no rules. Nor was it entirely unregulated. The lighting of a lantern on the wall and an oil lamp in a niche were the only routines followed on a daily basis. The layer of soot grew thicker by degrees as Kaka, oblivious to his surroundings and absorbed in his work, was completely lost in a world of invisible statues ready to birth under his fingers. Tapasi would sit quietly in her corner of the room. When he asked her, she would fetch water for him or raise the wick of the lamp. In between, she would watch him intently. Absorbed in work he seemed to be lost in a world of dreams. Often when he was busy working, a skein of saliva drooled from his thick lips. Tapasi would turn her face away in disgust at such moments. Between the extremes of aesthetic beauty and physical ugliness represented by Kaka, stood Tapasi whose existence seemed to be like those statues in the house. All they had was an impersonal sort of bond between them. The house belonged to Rakhal Kaka and she lived there. That was all.

Rakhal had little inclination towards speech or conversation. When he spoke, words seemed to tumble clumsily from his mouth. Tapasi often wondered why his words sounded so harsh. Whenever he was hungry he would sit cross-legged on a low wooden stool in the kitchen. Tapasi served him whatever she was able to cook—boiled rice, fish, machherjhol, dhakardalna in a thaali and placed it before him. Dinner over, he would unroll a mat in a corner and sleep on it. It was Tapasi who covered him with a sheet to keep off flies and mosquitoes. Worn out with the day's work and inebriated with toddy, Rakhal slept like a log. If he slept at night, Tapasi would too. Otherwise, she would come out and sit under the banyan tree in the courtyard.

The banyan tree was the focal point of the house. It stretched out like a canopy forming a shady roof over the house, as if it was holding the tiny family in its arms. Hundreds of tangled aerial roots sprang from its branches and hung to the ground. Sometimes, Tapasi would swing from them. At other times she would play hide and seek with imaginary characters in the dappled shade of the tree. The song of the birds flitting on the tree was her escape from the silence of the house. Carried away by birdsong, she would repeat the things her teacher did or her classmates had said. She would also revise her lessons to the tune of the birdsong. Watching the birds flitting in the courtyard was her entertainment. The fluttering of their colourful plumage inspired her to dance every now and then. Her own life had no connection with colours. All she had was a printed blue sari and a plain, dull blue blouse to wear to school. She had no saris like the ones Kanika Di wore. She knew she was poor.

Rakhal Kaka also had just a few sets of shabby clothes which Tapasi washed carefully to make respectable. Kaka moved in a circuit quite detached from Tapasi and any of her desires. She had no one remotely like a parental figure in her life. All she had was total loneliness, like a lone fish swimming in a pond.

Rakhal Kaka would get up in the morning and step out and smoke a bidi standing under the banyan tree. Then he proceeded to the courtyard where Tapasi would have already filled up a bucket of water for him. He took his bath sitting on a small platform without taking off his dhoti and vest. After the bath he would go back to his room and change into fresh clothes and put on his shoes, which he only wore when he went out. He would leave the house without a word and very often return after a day or two, at all odd hours. Tapasi had no information about where he went and when he would be back.

The sun rises and sets at fixed times, the moon swims silently into the sky on dark nights and plays hide and seek with the clouds but Rakhal's lifestyle had no concern with their regularity. Whatever he did was according to his own schedule. Tapasi had got quite used to staying by herself in the house. When Kaka returned from such absences he'd come with a bullock-cart full of shapeless rocks which were unloaded in a corner of the courtyard. Sometimes he brought back an attractive, buxom young woman with him. Tapasi thought that the woman's mannerisms, her style of dressing and her chunky silver jewellery, were quite unusual. Kaka would lead her into the room where she would smile, laugh and disrobe quite unselfconsciously. Mostly this happened behind closed doors but at times Kaka couldn't care less where Tapasi was. She would then watch in wonder as

Kaka's hands explored the nude figure of the woman for God knows what. He seemed to measure the outlines of her body and compute something on its basis. Maybe he was trying to divine something about the woman and she was not permitted to disturb him.

Tapasi watched the two of them in fascination. If the woman spoke, laughed or even coughed, Kaka would thrash her brutally. Alternatively, he would send the woman to stand at a distance and begin to run his chisel on a rock. Tapasi would watch the figure of the woman being replicated in stone by degrees. This process went on for days leading eventually to the creation of a brand new sculpture.

All this time, Tapasi also went regularly to school. She took care of household chores and read her books in the thatched veranda. She chopped vegetables, lit a fire in the hearth, boiled rice, cooked vegetables and served meals intermittently to Rakhal and the woman. Sometimes, Rakhal chose to close the door. When it opened, Kaka and the woman would emerge adjusting their clothes hurriedly. Laughing mysteriously, the woman would tie a large amount of money in the pallu of her sari. She would look at Tapasi with a smile and depart with her ankle bells tinkling. Kaka did not go back to work once she left. Without looking at Tapasi, he would place a few currency notes on the mat for household expenses and stuff the rest in his pocket. Subsequently, he either lay down and slept on the mat or went out.

Tapasi's childish mind was unable to comprehend the nature of the arrangement and the cash transaction between the woman and Rakhal. She would keenly examine the nude statue standing inside the room. It looked so life-like—smiling like the one who had rustled past her not so long ago. "But where has she gone," she would wonder. "Has she vanished forever in all these rocks?"

Living with Kaka, Tapasi had learnt to stay silent for long stretches of time. But her mind was always consumed with curiosity about her identity. Once Rakhal Kaka had told her that an English businessman had brought her father to him. But that was about all.

Rakhal's ancestors had carved sculptures in the caves of Ajanta and Ellora in the remote past. Their fame had spread up to Govindpur where they had been relocated around the time that Tagore Baba had founded Vishwa Bharti at Bolepur. That was during the time the British administrators visited Kolkata regularly. Under their influence, the name of the Thakur family was anglicized to Tagore. The Tagores were an honoured and distinguished family not only in Bengal but in all of India. The family was not only educated but gifted with far-sightedness and an inner vision which enabled them to understand the significance of a transitional, revolutionary epoch. That was the creed of those times. Under the patronage of aristocrats and rich feudal families, Rakhal's ancestors were engaged to further refine their skills.

Rakhal had no information about his zodiac sign, his *gotra* or the glorious history of his ancestors. But Jatin Dada had said on one occasion that Rakhal's forefathers must definitely have done something wrong while carving the statues of the Budhha, to punish which an ugly and ill-tempered man like Rakhal was born into their family. To that observation, Rakhal had answered with a wry smile, 'I may not be physically attractive, but my fingers can create beauty.'

On occasions when Jatin Dada brought a customer to Rakhal, he would beat a hasty retreat from the room, reeling under the fumes of toddy. He would then grumble, 'That is this man's obsession. He cannot work or live without toddy.' Rakhal's eyes would grow redder and he would guffaw at Jatin Dada's comment. Jatin Dada would scold him as he stroked the hair of little Tapasi standing close by. He would then say affectionately, 'Apart from art, the only beautiful thing in this house is Taposhi.'

'She is the daughter of my elder sister. Had I not rescued her under the cover of darkness, she too would be dancing with ghunghroos tied to her ankles instead of attending school. My sister's life is ruined. I may not be a perfect human being but I am committed to educating Taposhi and giving her a life of dignity. That is all.'

'You talk so much sense at times, Rakhal. This child is so intelligent. With the blessings of Ma, she will certainly be an achiever.'

Tapasi cherished this little anecdote relating to her birth and her mother's identity. Going religiously to school everyday, reading her books and pondering over what Teacher Didi said, she grew to be wiser than her years. Kanika Di and Jatin Da were the ones who'd insisted that she go to school. Jatin Da was a professor and Kanika Di a home-maker. They had a son, Malay. Watching him, Tapasi used to think that she would have to learn to fly to reach him and before she did that, she would need to learn to stand. She was still in the process of finding her feet when Malay went to study abroad.

Jatin Da was involved in the marketing of Rakhal's statues. He probably got a commission on the sales. That was the basis of his interaction with Rakhal. Kanika Di had taught Tapasi everything from wiping her nose to dressing properly. Malay had gone abroad. Tapasi wondered if 'abroad' ever sent people back to their homes. Building bridges between her uncertain situation and her dependence on Kanika Di, she continued to grow up. Time does not stand still. It leads individuals from place to place into an unknown future. She sought answers to all the questions crowding her mind from Jatin Da and Kanika Di. They were her answer to everything, a destination she had access to. She knew no world beyond theirs. Jatin Da used to call her 'Prashna' because she was perpetually and intensely eager to learn and know everything. Sometimes, when she went up to the bank of the river with Kanika Di, she wondered why the farthest point of the river seemed to merge with the distant sky stretched upon the earth. There was nothing at the point where water, earth and sky met. She had learnt in school that vacuum is where nothing exists. Did that mean that it was a vacuum?

Tapasi had a brilliant mind and could instantly comprehend the words her teachers uttered. Each lesson in school sank deep into her being as if all that she learnt was gradually filling up the deep void within her. As a child, Tapasi was fascinated by stories about kings and queens. A favourite was the one about the Emperor's New Clothes. She loved it when the guileless child spoke the truth about the Emperor's nakedness, laughing and free of fear. After listening to the story, the word 'truth' had got firmly embedded in Tapasi's self. She internalised it along with the other lessons she learnt from her textbooks.

◆◆◆

Once Kanika Di took Tapasi with her out of town. They went for a darshan of Ma Tara of Tara Peeth. Tapasi was thrilled at the prospect of going on a journey. Clutching Kanika Di's hand, she boarded a very crowded bus, full of all kinds of people. The speed of the bus thrilled her. She used to watch cars, tongas, bicycles and bullock-carts on the roads of Bolepur but she had never touched or boarded any of them. The sensation of sitting on a cushioned seat in a vehicle, and holding her head out of the window as the wind whooshed by, was unimaginably wonderful to her.

Kanika Di told her that they were going to a village which had once been called Ratna. She said that, once upon a time, a small spoke had detached itself from Sri Krishna's Sudarshan Chakra and fallen into the eye of Sati Devi Ma, who lived there. Now a temple had been put up there in her honour. The village grew into a town and the residents initially named it 'Tarapore' but later it became 'Tara Peeth'. Hordes of people visited the place to have darshan of Ma. Their faith grew and grew because of the spoke from Sri Krishna's Sudarshan Chakra being in Ma's eye which, no doubt, gave her divine powers.

Tapasi got off the bus clutching Kanika Di's pallu tightly. She was curious, astonished, ecstatic and frightened at the same time. Walking through the bazaar, she was dazzled by the crowded street and the colourful merchandise displayed in the shops. 'Oh Ma! What a lot of colours! What beautiful, shiny saris!' she exclaimed as she followed Kanika Di, anxious not to get separated from her.

After asking for directions, Kanika Di and she reached the main entrance of the temple. It was a magnificent door adorned by statues in different postures. The statues looked familiar to Tapasi. They bore some similarity to the statues sculpted by Kaka.

'Come, Taposhi. Where are you? Hurry up and do Ma's darshan otherwise the doors of the temple will close. It is almost midday.'

'Yes, Didi,' she said, emerging from behind her like a shadow. Kanika Di stood in front of the covered idol of Ma. She pulled the pallu of her sari over her head and bowed over and over again, then prostrated herself on the floor. Tapasi mimicked her gestures as closely as she could, in all the attitudes of worship. Suddenly, the temple priest pulled the red curtain that screened the idol, to reveal the Goddess. Tapasi gasped at the exquisite golden figure with cascading black hair that stood in front of them, staring at it in wide-eyed wonder.

Kanika Di took out the sweets, fruits and flowers she had brought with her in a cloth bag and arranged them in a basket. She repeated a jaap softly as she extended her basket towards the priest who pulled it in and closed the curtain once again. Inside, he tinkled the bell he was holding in his hand and recited some mantras in a loud voice. Subsequently, he pronounced, '*Ma hey ma, teri jai ho*', and pulled the curtain apart once more. Tapasi was awestruck. She was sure that Ma would have eaten half of the fruits and sweets in that time but the whole offering lay untouched in front of her. The priest took half of it and thrusting the other half in Kanika Di's hands, called out to the next worshipper in the queue.

After doing the darshan they came into the outer courtyard of the temple through the exit door where a few sadhus sat. Kanika Di went up to them, pulled the pallu of her sari over her head and prostrated herself before them. Tapasi quickly followed suit. A sage-like gentleman, standing close by said, 'Do you know, Ma, that both Sri Ramakrishna Paramhansa and Sri Bamkhepa were the favoured devotees of Ma Bhagwati by whose grace we cross the ocean of life safely.'

One of the sadhus asked, 'Do you know anything about Sri Bamkhepa, the ascetic of the cremation ground of Tara Peeth?'

'No, I don't, Maharaj,' Kanika Di answered.

'When he calls out to Tara Ma, his voice reverberates through the cosmos,' the gentleman said.

'How does that happen?' Kanika Di trembled in fear and excitement.

'His call can be heard every night. He resides in the cremation ground. Ma, you can hear his voice rising above the burning pyres at midnight.'

'Can ordinary mortals like us hear that voice?' Kanika Di was keen to know.

'Yes, of course they can. But you'll have to stay overnight.'

'Let us stay back tonight, Taposhi. It will be a new experience for us.'

It was then about four in the afternoon. The sanyasi who had spoken to them sent another man in saffron robes to guide them. They were led to a spacious hall with a marble floor and rooms on both sides. Tapasi had never seen such a clean floor in her life. She wanted to touch it—it was so white and smooth. The saffron clad gentleman opened the lock of one of the rooms and left. Inside the room was a wooden divan covered with a sheet with a floral print. A chair stood by the divan. Tapasi was surprised to see so much furniture in such a small room.

Kanika Di took off her shawl, folded it and put it away. She lay down and relaxed on the divan. Making room for Tapasi on the side, she said, 'Come, lie down. You must be tired.'

'What does tired mean, Didi?'

'Don't you feel a physical strain, Taposhi? I'm completely exhausted after that bumpy bus ride.'

'No, Didi. All this is so new to me....' She was at a loss for words. Her mind was crowded with questions about her new experiences. A faint but pleasant thrill went through her body as she stretched herself on the soft, thick mattress on the divan. It was so different from her frayed jute mat back home. She couldn't help saying, 'What a lovely place to sleep in! Does the house of Ma have such rooms for everybody?'

'You are so innocent, Taposhi. This is a bed with a cotton mattress. People sleep on mattresses in every home.'

'And how about the floor outside?'

'That floor is made of marble which is a kind of rock. Your Kaka carves statues out of sandstone. Marble is also used in sculpture. Most white statues are made of it. You get green and black marble too.'

'Oh!' Tapasi exclaimed. She fell silent and soon went off to sleep. It was evening when Didi woke her up. The saffron robed sanyasi stood before them with two leaf plates piled high with food. Kanika spread a newspaper and placed the plates on it. 'Come and eat, Taposhi. You must be hungry.'

For Tapasi it was unfamiliar food—puri, bhaji, pickle, sweets. She observed Kanika Di eating and, copying her, broke off a bit of the puri, wrapped it around the bhaji and put it in her mouth. Savoury, pungent, sweet—so many sensations of taste! She was putting them, layer by layer, in the store-house of her experiences. The flavours were so exotic, so new. She realized she had been experiencing a slew of new sensations—visual, gastronomic and tactile—since she had come to Tara Peeth.

At nightfall, the two of them followed the sanyasi out of the temple premises. It had stopped raining but a light drizzle dampened their clothes. The city seemed to fall asleep early. Lights had already begun to be switched off in the rest-house. Holding each other's hands, they followed the faint light of the lantern the sanyasi was carrying. Stopping at an intersection, he spoke to a pedestrian briefly and then moved on. He said nothing to them throughout the way. Kanika Di asked a few questions which he did not answer. Their feet sank into the mud. At one point, Kanika Di pressed Tapasi's hand and asked, 'Are you scared?'

'Not a bit,' Tapasi answered cheerfully.

The sanyasi turned to look at her carefully for the first time since they'd got there. 'Oh Ma! How extraordinary!' His grave, bass voice startled both Tapasi and Kanika Di.

"And what does extraordinary mean?" A question again. "Why can't I understand things," Tapasi wondered. Then taking courage in both her hands, she pressed on, 'Baba, if one does not know anything about life, what should one do? How does one understand life?'

'You are too innocent for today's world, Didi Ma. You should read good books. You'll learn much through them. Keep good company, converse with decent people. You have a pure heart—like a sanyasi,' he answered gently.

They walked on. After a while they stopped talking and walked in silence. Finally, the sanyasi stopped and said, 'This is *aatla*, Didi Ma. The cremation ground is on the left. Take this lantern and sit on the platform under the silk cotton tree. You'll definitely hear the voice of Bamkhepa.'

Kanika Di took the lantern and bravely did what the sanyasi had suggested. She started a jaap. Turning to Tapasi, she said, 'Taposhi, you too should do the jaap of Ma. Repeat, "Ma, Tara Ma" all the way.'

'I will,' answered Tapasi and immediately took up the chant even though her mind was crowded with questions. "What is a cremation ground? What is a jaap? And Ma?

Why don't I have a mother? Other girls in school do. They talk about their Ma and Baba all the time. How come I have only Kaka?"

The drizzle stopped. Kanika Di said, 'Do you see those burning coals in the distance? And the smoke? Do you know what they are? But, of course you don't know. Let me tell you...well...that is a pyre....'

'What is a pyre?' Tapasi couldn't contain her curiousity.

'I knew you were going to ask a question. Your Dada is right. Your name should have been 'Prashna', the one who asks questions! When a person dies his body is brought here for cremation which is performed by placing the body on a pile of wood and setting it on fire. Wait, wait. Now don't ask me what death is. People who die leave the world forever. Like your father.'

'Did you know him?'

'No, I didn't. But look, Sanyasi Baba is going back leaving us alone!'

'Didi, when we came here there was only one lantern between us. How come now he has another one with him?'

But Kanika did not answer her questions. She resumed her jaap instead.

Namo namo ambe dukh harni, namo namo ambe sukh karni, nirankar hai jyoti tumhari, tihun loke phaili ujiyari.

Suddenly the stillness of the night was broken by the sound of a deep sonorous voice proclaiming: 'Hey Tara Ma'.

Kanika trembled as copious tears rolled down her cheeks. Tapasi held her hand and repeated her name. She was quite calm and unruffled herself.

◆◆◆

Morning crept in unknown to Tapasi. She did not know whether she had just been sitting around and fallen asleep or whether she had passed out. When she woke, she found herself and Didi alone. A couple of birds flitted around the few trees in the cremation ground.

They came out of the straw and bamboo enclosure and found Sanyasi Baba waiting for them. Wordlessly they fell in behind him. There was no evidence of last night's rain and slush. The path was completely dry. Had they taken a different route last night? They stopped outside a house with a tubewell from which water flowed freely. They washed their feet and shoes, both of which were coated with mud from the night before. Sanyasi Baba introduced them to a gentleman who, he said, was one of Bamkhepa's descendants. They had lived in the house since the sage's time. According to Sanyasi Baba everyone dropped by to pay their respects drawn by Bamkhepa's voice.

Soon after, a woman brought two thaalis of food for them. They ate well. Kanika felt blessed—as if she had partaken of the bhog of the noble souls by whose blessings she had had the divine experience. Tapasi's thoughts followed another trail. She just believed she had never eaten such delicious food before.

As they took their leave and began walking on, they noticed a group of men doing *Chandi Paath* in the cremation ground. The road bore no evidence of last night's rain. Kanika was truly overwhelmed and tears welled up in her eyes. Tapasi wondered why she was crying after such a beautiful experience. She tried to console and comfort Didi as they both did *pranaam* to the house before coming back out onto the road.

'Come on, Didi, we have a long way to go,' Tapasi said, then turning to Sanyasi Baba, she asked, 'Could you please take us to the bus terminal?'

'Yes, of course,' he answered.

Tapasi looked longingly at the merchandise on display in the shops as they passed through the Bazaar street. There were heaps of sindoor, colourful hair bands, small idols of Ma, books, terracotta toys, all manner of things.

'Didi, I want to buy a copybook,' Tapasi said suddenly, on a whim, taking out some money she had knotted into the pallu of her sari.

'Sure,' Kanika Di said, 'but what will you write in it? School work?'

'Yes...among other things.'

Tapasi was delighted. She bought a big blue exercise book for ten rupees. She realized that she had just experienced something extraordinary and she needed a notebook to record and preserve the memory of it. She could write down the questions that rose in her mind all the time. What is fear? Why do some people wear saffron robes? What was the best part of this trip—the bus ride, the darshan of Tara Ma, or the continuous journey of discovery within herself?

It was late evening by the time they reached the Bolepur bus terminal. The sky was turning a deep blue and dusk was shortly to descend. Tapasi was worried about Rakhal Kaka. Suppose he had come home? He would be hungry and cross. He would flare up just seeing her. As it was, she took long to cook. It was difficult to start the kitchen fire with damp wood. The thatched roof leaked during the rains and drove her crazy.

Tapasi preferred the sun to the rain. The sun dried the firewood and the wash. It guided her to school on time. She also liked the moon even though it was much paler than the sun. She remembered how a dull moon had kept them company between the bus terminals of Bamkhepa and Bolepur. Each time that she'd walked the road that led to the grove of silk, cotton and flame-of-the forest trees, was special to her. She was always struck by the magnificent statue of Tagore Baba there. Whenever she had the time she went there to gaze at the statue, and, overwhelmed by the sight of it, would lose herself in a world of dreams. Jatin Da had told her that Vishwa Bharti, the sprawling university, was Rabindranath Tagore's brainchild. The institution, situated in Bolepur, the city of red soil, had been his magnificent obsession. Jatin Da also told her that Tagore Baba had invested all his resources—financial, intellectual and spiritual—in the construction of this university. He was like a potter, Jatin Da said, blending his being in the form of drops of water, using it to moisten the clay to mould pots from it at his wheel.

Apparently, or so the legend goes, Tagore Baba once stood on the roof of Shantiniketan and surveyed the tall trees on Vishwa Bharti's campus grounds. A number of trees grew there—Sal, Chhatim, Mahua, Maulsri, Laburnum and Mango—but only the branches of the Sal seemed to sing a song of affinity with his heart. Watching them, he felt his financial worries and technical problems relating to the construction of the building, disappear, allowing him to freely envision the university taking shape there. He was deeply inspired by this vision and devoted all his energies to realizing it.

Returning to the world of reality, he understood that the Sals were not just trees, they were a silent hymn to the spirit of the earth. They were hands raised in prayer, a prayer which resonated through all phenomena and drenched it with holiness. And their song was enriched by the spontaneous and joyous laughter of children at play. A spirit of freedom and boundless wisdom seemed to rise from the earth to blend with the slowly falling dusk. There is nothing greater than Nature, and Nature herself seemed to whisper words of inspiration, like a Puranic seer, in his ears…

'*Kahanyevanyat ka prashyat yadesh aakash anando na syat*'

(Had not the whole sky been swaying with love, who would ever be able to struggle and survive in this world?)

These words were strong enough to overcome all the impediments in his path. The difficulties in the construction of Vishwa Bharti were smoothly sorted out. Work done for universal good generates exquisite spiritual energy. Faith, and a life of integrity, become a part of universal truth. Tagore Baba felt a current of self-confidence run through him. And Vishwa Bharti began to acquire a concrete form, rising out of the red earth of Bolepur.

Jatin Da told Tapasi about what a unique university it was. It did not impose a rigid curriculum upon its students. Its most striking feature was its environment, its natural surroundings. Its very structure and its tree filled gardens taught harmony with Nature. It was not a college but an ashram residing where one got the sense of having obtained citizenship of the divine kingdom of God.

Living close to Nature, one cannot but admire the grandeur of the sun and moon. Observing flowers bloom and trees come to fruition, one spontaneously realizes one's humanity. Doors of knowledge open on their own. Teachers and students of all ages sit together and eat at the same table. The food is not just the stuff of subsistence. It serves to nourish inner spiritual needs as well. The very trees in the gardens cascade joy in the form of birdsong through the day.

Tapasi grew up cherishing the idea of Vishwa Bharti in her heart. It shared a sacred place along with innumerable other memories. Memories of Ma at Tara Peeth, of still smouldering pyres in the cremation ground, of the exquisite food she had eaten at Bamkhepa—but best of all, of the ground on which Tagore Baba had walked, the sky, which must have been the base of his dreams, the trees, coming up in answer to the prayers of so many people, the long stretch of barren land devoid of flowers or foliage, the iron gate in the distance—the barely visible rooftops of the Shantiniketan ashram concealed by thick groves of toddy and date palm which stood like the columns of an ancient monument. Inside, under a Chhatim tree, was the rock on which Maharishi Devendranath had prayed during one of his journeys. His prayer was for the founding of a temple where people of all faiths could worship. There was an inscription on the rock which read, 'He is the repose of my life, the joy of my mind and the peace of my soul.'

Tapasi wasn't sure whether she was awake or dreaming, but a few moments from the past had conveyed so much to her. What was it all if not a dream? Jatin Da's words, an imagined conversation, or a disembodied voice?

Walking in a trance-like state, she'd found herself before a small house plastered with clay bearing the name 'Shyamali'. Someone had told her that Tagore Baba had spent the last days of his life here. A modest abode for someone so great. A wooden board displayed the following verse:

'I have built with mud a shelter for my last hour
And named it Shyamali.
I have built it on that dust
Which buries in it all sufferings,
And cleanses all stains.'

Baba had surrendered his last days to the dust, which set him free from all suffering and winged him to an immaculate life. Tapasi had copied the inscription into her blue book. She was experiencing a new kind of joy, as if her whole being was etched with unforgettable sensations. As she was absorbing all the new sensations, a sudden gust of wind covered her with dust, but this did not upset her. Instead, she was overwhelmed by the feel of the rich heritage of the place. She walked through the dust storm past the various sites of the university. The 'Kala Bhawan', where Nandlal Bose's black and white visual depictions of Tagore's poetry were on display; 'Udayan', where Tagore Baba resided for some time and where his handwritten and illustrated manuscripts were preserved in a treasure-house of Tagore memorabilia. Amazed and curious, Tapasi had lingered there for a long while. She wondered who had brought her there. How had she reached this place? And how fulfilling and uplifting the whole experience had been! She walked on, in that enchanted state, to a grove of Sal trees whose solitude seemed to resonate with the poems of Tagore Baba. Each stone, each wall of the place, echoed with the sound of the morning prayer, the *Vaitalik*.

She returned home in the silence of night. The door was open. Kaka was engrossed in his work. He did not notice her. Tapasi watched fascinated as in the faint light of the oil lamp he added the final touches to perfect the figure he had been working on, giving it its defining finish. Fine movements, which, like subtle feelings, refine our sensibility. How did he do it? Tapasi was becoming Prashna once again.

JATIN DA RESIDED in a small house at the far end of a road lined by shady Chahal trees. The house had a red roof that set it apart from the bustle of the basti. He had some creepers in his garden, which were perennially in bloom. 'There is a yellow smell in the air,' Tapasi would say much to the mirth of Kanika Di who would laugh, 'You funny girl! Do you think smells have colours?'

'So how does smell manifest itself?'

'Oh God! This girl is impossible. Run off now.' Kanika Di would get exasperated by her persistent queries but Jatin Da would explain to her, 'Taposhi, scents are smelt and felt.

You cannot see them. It is like sensing the good and bad qualities of people.'

God knows how much sense she made of such explanations but she loved going to their house. Tapasi admired Kanika Di's style of dressing. The elegant way she draped her sari, the sindoor she sprinkled in the parting of her hair and the large bindi on her forehead. She looked so attractive.

Tapasi seemed to blend in with the family and the day-to-day routine of their household. The drawing room was neat and well-furnished with sofas and chairs. The kitchen was alive with the bustle and clatter of vessels being washed and food being cooked. Jatin Da was an impressive and popular man. Many Indian and foreign visitors and colleagues visited their house and dropped in of an evening. Sophisticated gatherings of distinguished people. The lone retainer of the household, who was cook, gardener and watchman rolled into one, would fetch Tapasi whenever guests were expected. Tapasi would come promptly and eagerly and take over from Kanika Di. She fried the bhajias, garnished the gurer sandesh with ilaichidana and poured tea into cups. She would arrange the snacks prettily on a large tray and carry it out to the guests. She loved all the fancy machines and gadgets in the house.

She thought of Jatin Da's house as an ideal home, enriched by the presence of its residents and all their visitors—the conversation, and the free and frank discussions, which she listened to attentively, hiding in a corner of the drawing room. On such occasions, Tapasi marvelled all the more at Jatin Da's personality and character. Shedding his sombre, dignified persona, he would participate in the discussions with the animated fervour of a seventeen-year-old. His talk was always lively and he held forth with authority on every subject under the sun. The others in the gathering were enthralled by his engaging manner and their parties were famous for the exuberant and lively discussions that followed the meals. Jatin Da's nostrils would flare and the pain in his chronically aching back would miraculously ease when he spoke. His forehead shone as if illumined from within. Tapasi was intimidated by the lofty wisdom of these discussions—discussions about big, fat books that were strewn all over the room and from which they would read from time to time. They talked about painting and music and a whole lot of other things that were perfectly incomprehensible to her.

Then one day, an unusual event took place in the small lawn of Jatin Da's house. Tapasi saw Indian and foreign guests standing on one side of the lawn while on the other sat some musicians with a one-string lute, a dafli and a mridanga. One man wore ghunghroos on his feet. In time, the guests occupied the chairs and sat down on the dhurries intended for them. Kanika Di had arranged trays full of puffed rice ladoos, coconut naadus and other goodies at strategic places. Tapasi was looking after the guests with her usual enthusiasm.

Refreshments over, Jatin Da introduced the party of singers to the audience. He said they were Vaishnavas and they sang Baul songs. Baul was a regional style folk-music and dance that represented their traditions and philosophy of life.

The performance commenced. Everyone was spellbound. Tapasi sat mesmerized in a corner, listening and watching in rapt attention. The music transported her to another world. Where that world was she did not know? The words of the song and the music created a kind of space around them. The man with the ghunghroos on his feet danced with graceful feminine movements. He would lift his hands to illustrate a scene and conveyed emotions through his eyes so eloquently that they sank deep into the hearts of the spectators.

O kaancha haandi te rakhite narili prem jal
Kaancha haandi jaky diley tenakhoni jaeehey goley
takhontor jeeboney laagbey gandagoh
O re man hobi jodi paaka haandi
jao guru kumarer baadi
Tarvontor wopetey korbey talomah
Guru Shadanando bhebey aauul.
Khaipa manohar ki hobi baul.
Dekh dekh dekh dhaan kutiley haibe chauul
Toosh kutiley ki ba phal!

(You have not been able to store the water of love in an unbaked clay pot. It is but natural that an unbaked pot would crumble into a clod of clay if you put water into it.

Such an act creates a wrangle in your life. O my heart, you'll have to go to the house of the master potter if you want to be a perfect clay pot. He is the one who would refine you into resplendent beauty. Even Sadanand Guru gets into a frenzy at such ideas and thoughts, so how could a modest Manohar Bad remain untouched by them? Look, look, we obtain rice only after pounding paddy. We cannot possibly reap a harvest from straw).

'The quest for truth is the central aspect of the mystique of India's philosophical tradition. Our value system is as integral to regional folklore and music as flowers are to a garland,' Jatin Da explained to a friend. 'These ancient ditties are an exposition of cultural studies in colloquial language.'

Tapasi dwelt on a line from the song. *Tor roopetey korbey talomal.* She would also aspire to refine herself into a resplendent beauty—of character and of mind.

One of the guests, a Japanese woman named Maki Kazumi, who was studying Bengali at Vishwa Bharti as part of her research on Tagore, began to repeat the Baul song in broken Bengali. Then she laughed self-consciously and said, *'Kharap, Kharapl'* Her flat nose looked flatter and her eyes crinkled and disappeared into the lines of her face as she laughed. She had such an unusual face. Tapasi wondered at the sheer variety of faces and facial expressions around her. Serious, happy, angry, grimacing, curious—like the colourful masks sold in the market. Some faces had eyes that looked but didn't see—large, glazed eyes. But the Japanese woman seemed to see everything with her small, slanting ones. She had come all the way from Japan to do research on Tagore Baba. Tapasi remembered that Teacher Didi had once told her that Vishwa Bharti was a place where people from the whole world were welcome. It was an open house to which anybody could come.

Everybody, including the folk singers, laughed at Maki Kazumi's efforts to speak Bengali. Tapasi, who was serving tea and snacks to the guests, too found it very funny. She put down the tray, sat down on the floor and began to laugh aloud.

Immediately, Kanika Di came over and pulled her up, 'O Ma! Taposhi, will you behave yourself? This is a gathering of civilized people. Should you laugh here in such an uncouth manner?'

Tapasi froze. She had always enjoyed a lot of freedom and spontaneity in this house, but now suddenly she felt like a caged animal in a zoo. "Am I one of Kaka's statues, allowed only a fixed smile on my face? Why can't I laugh spontaneously? What is so uncouth about laughing naturally? I did not know that laughter too had degrees and layers. What is civilized laughter? Am I not civilized? Why can't I laugh like the others? Why should I keep quiet? I am not a servant like Bholanath. But then, what am I doing here?" She could follow the talk and discussion in the gatherings.

She understood the meaning of the Baul songs. She was studying in a school. Her teachers thought her intelligent.

She left the party and rushed home feeling utterly miserable. As soon as she reached home, she sensed that Kaka was fuming about something. He had been in a temper for quite some time, his anger abetted by toddy. He unleashed it on Tapasi, further demolishing what remained of her shattered dreamworld. After a couple of tight slaps, Tapasi returned to the world of reality. A world which had nothing to offer by way of books, poetry and the yellow perfume of flowers.

Tapasi started cooking hastily as he raved and ranted, 'Where did you go? I've been famished for so long. Don't you know that I can't work till I've eaten and can't breathe properly till I've drunk toddy? How do you expect me to start my work? There is a new buyer. He is pressurizing me to hurry up,' he shouted as he showered blows on her.

Tapasi quickly set down a plate of sliced onions and roasted papads in front of him. After he ate them and washed them down with toddy, he mellowed somewhat.

'I did not want you to go your mother's way, that is why I brought you here. I worry about you when you go out at night. When I am away, you sleep alone in the house. Don't you feel scared, Taposhi?'

She looked at him in disbelief. Kaka, concerned about her? How come the heart of the one who sculpted stone statues, stirred for her?

A man on the brink of oblivion sometimes speaks the truth. Truths buried deep within oneself come to the fore in a state of inebriation. Kaka stared at Tapasi cooking machher jhol and rice. She was wondering what fear meant and how it was associated with night or outdoors. The only definable feeling of fear she was familiar with was the one she felt when she stood before him after being summoned to his presence. Looking at him at such times was like brushing against the cold steel of an executioner's sword.

He did not lift his hand again till after he finished the bottle of toddy. Then he chucked the empty bottle aside and kicked Tapasi who was sitting near the stove. In a while, he flopped on the mat spread out on the floor and began to throw up. An overpowering stink pervaded the house. Leaving the rice boiling on the stove, Tapasi helped him get up and led him to the water tap where she washed and cleaned his body. In the process, she also went back to remove the pot of rice from the stove and rushed to the drain near the tile-roofed veranda to vomit her own bitterness out.

Rakhal recovered a bit after a while. He ate the rice, lay down, rolled over and fell asleep. Tapasi ate a frugal meal of rice and jaggery. After washing up, she settled down to write in her diary by the light of the oil lamp. The episode at Jatin Da's house came slithering back into her mind. All the people there ate and drank in a seemly way. No one slapped and kicked her. But Kanika Di said she was uncivilized. One should laugh properly. Laughter has layers and degrees. Serenity and nobility pervaded Kanika Di's house but they were totally absent here. Kanika Di was right. But she was the one who had taught her everything. Tapasi was confused. She wondered if her identity was no better than that of a cockroach crawling in a corner of the house—to be crushed underfoot at will. If this was true, then why? She had trusted Kanika Di so completely. Were faith and trust fickle things? A sense of acute loneliness enveloped her. She realized that she would have to search for her identity, her life, and her chances in life all by herself. Why was she not considered civilized? Why did Kaka thrash her? What had she done to deserve such humiliating treatment?

There were innumerable stars in the night sky. Tapasi realized that she had never noticed before how clear and bright they looked. Maybe one of them was her mother's star. She wondered which one it was and whether it would redeem her from her plight and rescue her from the never-ending questions crowding her mind. Tapasi was not given to crying. She did not know what crying meant, or laughter, or fear. And what it meant to be civilized. Poor Tapasi did not know a thing. Surrounded by her questions and still feeling hollow inside, she was unable to write anything in her notebook and when she curled up in bed, she fell into a restless sleep.

ON HER WAY back from school, Tapasi always walked by Didi's tea-stall, which was crowded with students at all times, her feet slowing themselves of their own volition, as she approached. She loved looking at all the young people with files and books in their hands, many of whom were white-skinned foreigners. They conversed and laughed animatedly over cups of tea and argued and debated endlessly. Once she'd gone and stood nearer to the crowd than usual. A personal dream, pristine, white like a heron, stretched before her. Most of the faces she saw were happy, laughing faces. She wanted to study each face to assess who laughed in a civilized manner and whose manner was uncouth like hers. Did laughter signify an identity or a circumstance? She did not know. Teacher Didi never laughed. She always had a straight face, a sombre mask, which had to do with teaching subjects related to education and nothing else. Kanika Di had told her that Teacher Didi was a Christian and she was not married. Tapasi wondered if all Christian faces looked like the masks sold at the Pausb Mela. Jatin Da had used the word 'spinster' for her. Was a spinster one of those characters who stepped out of the realm of fiction into the plays performed during Durga Puja?

Anyway, Tapasi really loved Didi's tea-stall. It filled

her with inspiration and a yearning for the unknown. She imagined that she too would come here to study when she grew up. She would hold big, heavy books in her hands and converse with her fellow students—even with the foreign ones. And yes, she would laugh. A gentle, civilized laugh, which wouldn't be a mask but her own laughter. Free and spontaneous.

Another place that she yearned to visit was the Chhatim Tila on the Vishwa Bharti campus. She'd visited it once with Teacher Didi and a friend of hers. They had gone to a small platform situated under a Chhatim tree. It was here that Thakur Dada's father had dreamt of establishing Vishwa Bharti. That dream had come true. As witness to that dream, the place was now a hallowed spot.

Teacher Didi said lightly, 'A lot of people who pretend to be intellectuals gather here to drink tea but the real intellectuals call them 'auntel' which is a corruption of intellectual. Visiting this place is a must for the elite and the self-proclaimed intellectuals who come here to show off. But few people come to bow here with reverence. Most who visit the place are pseudo-intellectuals who have nothing to do with literature or spirituality. Such people are ridiculous.'

'How often do you come here?' Teacher Didi's friend asked.

'As often as I can. Whenever time permits, I come and sit quietly here. I listen to the birds sing in the branches of the trees. I think that the birds sing either in praise of God, or just for themselves, but caged birds are compelled to sing to their captors. They sing in a business-like manner. In the same way, there is a difference in being an intellectual and a pseudo-intellectual. This Chhatim tree is witness to all those who come here wearing masks. They talk, laugh, show off and pose as intellectuals.'

The two of them burst out laughing. Teacher Didi with her ordinary features, her bindi-less face and her simply draped sari, and her friend who was as austere as she was, didn't conceal their faces behind masks, thought Tapasi. Was their decorous laughter—caught in the pallu of their saris pressed to their mouths, rather than carried by the breeze—'civilized' laughter?

◆◆◆

Someone had abandoned an old broken-down bullock-cart outside the fence of Rakhal's house. Tapasi would stand and observe it quietly on her way to and from school. She couldn't help feeling the bullock-cart wanted her to adopt it. One afternoon, with the help of Jatin Da's servant, Bholanath, she managed to push it inside her compound and install it under the banyan tree. Bholanath provided her with rope, reeds and straw with which she excitedly repaired and decorated the cart. Up until then, the only companion of her solitude was the banyan tree in the compound. The sun and shade peeking through its aerial roots and overhanging branches had formed the backdrop to all her pretend-play about imagined good and bad characters—brave kings who bound the bad guys with the roots and then flogged them, for instance. At other times, she enjoyed swinging on the roots and reciting poems learned at school, or the Baul songs she had heard at Jatin Da's house. It was wonderful to sit there during the rains but sometimes at night the tree assumed a menacing shape, which though it made her a little anxious never seriously frightened her. Her inquisitive mind still clamoured to understand the meaning of the word 'fear' that Rakhal Kaka had spoken to her about. "What is fear?" she often asked herself.

The broken down bullock-cart had been transformed into a wondrous retreat furnished with a straw mat and repaired and decorated with reeds and straw. Tapasi found great novelty and variety in her new enterprise. Some of her dreams escaped from her sleep and settled in and around the bullock-cart. Unfamiliar yearnings would inspire her to write all kinds of things in her notebook. Pieces on the rain, about the Japanese student, about Chhatim Tila. The Tila had made a deep impact on her. She would visit there again and again if she could. But when could she go? She hardly had any free time.

Tapasi had been most fascinated when Teacher Didi explained the anatomy of the human body to the class with the help of a real skeleton. Some of the girls had screamed on seeing the skeleton. Others had said they were scared out of their wits. But Tapasi felt nothing like fear. Gazing at the skeleton, the only feeling she had was one of amazement. For a long time she pondered how much deep study would be needed to unravel the mysteries of the human anatomy. Innumerable arteries and veins, blood, fluids, flesh, skin, organs—and the entire skeleton—there is so much that goes into forming a human body. Kaka's statues had bodies but no skeletons. Once, she had heard someone at Jatin Da's say, 'The body is made of clay ... all words, all sentences are subtle atoms and nuclei of the same clay. And our goal is to set ourselves free from it.'

Tapasi's mind was a vast treasure-house where everything she heard, saw or read was stored only to playback in her consciousness, like taped music.

On the evening of the day she had seen the skeleton, something seemed, literally, to snap inside her. Stained heavily with blood, she had rushed to Kanika Di's house. She thought she was dying and all the blood was oozing out of her body. "Was her life going to be flushed out of her body with the blood? Was she nearing the moment of her death?"

Before explaining anything, Kanika Di planted two slaps on her face for her ignorance and naivete. Then she led her into a room and closed the door. When she finally opened the door and let Tapasi out, Tapasi's eyes were downcast. Just as well Kaka was not home when she returned. He had gone to buy stone for a new statue. Tapasi made an entry on a new page in her blue notebook. 'Kanika Di says I am no longer a little girl. I have come of age.' She was electrified by the thought. What did it mean—to come of age?

THE STUDENTS OF Tapasi's school were shown movies from time to time. On one such occasion, a white screen was stretched across a wall. A machine with two spools was installed in front of it. Tapasi, her best friend, and the other girls of the school sat cross-legged on the dhurries spread out on the floor. Teacher Didi told them that they would be shown a newsreel first to be followed by a movie. All the girls sat down expectantly. Tapasi was all agog. The darkness and silence combined to intensify the tension in the air. Her friend whispered, 'Taposhi, I am so scared!'

As for Tapasi, she believed that certain things made your heart beat faster, but she still had no idea what fear meant.

After a while, the spools began to roll. The first thing to flash on the screen were the words 'The News', accompanied by subdued music and pictures of men and women flashing and receding on the screen. Ugly, bloated men with folded hands, described as leaders, inaugurating new factories and schools, people garlanding and felicitating them with high praise as others clapped and cheered. Shots of half-clad male and female labourers carrying baskets full of concrete mix on their heads at construction sites. Workers putting up a dam in flowing, deep waters. Others busy manufacturing goods on machines in factories with high walls. Machines yielding manufactured goods which were then packed into boxes. The thrill of seeing so much that was new to her gave Tapasi goosebumps. To see, to understand, and to store all that information in her mind was an amazing experience for her.

She was still feeling that thrill when a few skeletal figures appeared on the screen. The people who were shown had peculiarly shrivelled-up bodies and faces that looked distorted and scary. Most of the faces showed disproportionately large white teeth. Flies swarmed around the faces. The hands were too weak to wave them away, the bodies were emaciated. The pictures were profoundly disturbing. Tapasi's friend held her hand tightly and said, 'O Ma! Are they ghosts? Chase them away, please.' She closed her eyes, but Tapasi's eyes were focused on their empty bowls and the filth surrounding them. She shook off her friend's hand and answered, 'They are not ghosts. They are emaciated human beings or beggars like the ones who sit outside the temple of Devi Ma. Don't you see that they are holding begging bowls in their hands? Look—I think those children are dying of starvation.'

The voice of the invisible commentator said, 'This is Sudan. Sudan is in the grip of a severe drought. A large number of people are dying of starvation here everyday. Senior citizens of Sudan, who are protesting against the People's Liberation Army, are lying exposed to the sun outside the food distribution centre set up by Oxfam. They have grown so weak that they cannot even drag themselves to the shade under the trees. All their strength has been drained by hunger and thirst.'

The screen then showed countless thin, skeletal children with bloated abdomens and arms and legs that looked like twigs. They crawled whimpering over the ground. Their pitiable condition shook Tapasi to the core. Then she saw a white-skinned nurse feeding them with her hands. The newsreel also had a shot of half-naked women holding their children to their dried-up breasts and wandering through the night in search of food. A few naked men spoke about their plight. They had no homes, not a morsel of food. They were forced to spend the night under the trees. In order to sustain their families somehow, they were constrained to abandon the old and dying to the mercy of the elements, out in the open.

Tapasi began to weep. She had tears in her eyes for the first time. Her heart quaked and she felt anxious. She wondered if that was the feeling her friend called fear. After the film was over, she realized that she had experienced so much in a short while. Drought, starvation, naked men and women, skeletal forms, death. And then a foreign country, an alien city. Clutching a big bundle of new experiences to herself, she hurried home. She moved away from the bustle of the city to her own world—her banyan tree, her bullock-cart, her paddy, her cooked rice. The rains had stopped but there were puddles on both sides of the road. Ugly scum had formed on the surface of the stagnant water—scum that reminded her of the wasted bodies of the drought-stricken men and women of Sudan and Somalia. Tapasi was listening to echoes of new contexts delving deep into her consciousness. She had discovered a new word—'concern'. Concern about protection of humanity, concern about human dignity. She thought for a long time what action should be taken when one felt concerned about something.

OF LATE THE man with the white cap had started making frequent visits to Rakhal. Tapasi could see that these visits pleased Kaka a lot. Perhaps, because in the process of ordering and buying the statues, not only was he handsomely recompensed, but was also slipped a couple of toddy bottles. Tapasi had often caught the man staring intently at her as she went about her work or served him tea. There was something disconcerting about his gaze. The manner in which he plied Kaka with gifts filled Tapasi with a sense of foreboding. A confused Tapasi would seek refuge from them in her bullock-cart. She had realized that there were distinctions in the way different people looked at others. The man with the cap looked at, but did not see Kaka. And how about the way Kanika Di and Jatin Da looked at people? Theirs was an inquisitive gaze, which built bridges between one experience and another. As for her own gaze, she would usually stand at the threshold of a new experience with questions flashing out of her eyes. But the gaze of the man with the cap bore through the straw mat of the bullock-cart and into her back, making her shiver in disgust. It was an unpleasant, penetrating gaze that seemed to pierce her flesh even as she pulled the free end of her sari tighter around her. She was convinced that he was totally different from the visitors at Jatin Da's house. For some reason, she began to feel anxious about her future.

One day, when she went to Jatin Da's house she found the place bustling with festivity. She learnt that Malay, Kanika Di's son, had returned. Kanika Di's enthusiasm was infectious. She was busy making an *alpana* at the entrance and Tapasi was helping her by handing her the kumkum, roli and rice when she bumped into an exceedingly handsome young man who suddenly entered through the door. The thaali in Tapasi's hand fell onto the floor with a clatter. Kanika Di's voice admonished her, Taposhi, how come you walk around with your eyes closed?'

But Tapasi was lost to the world as she gazed hypnotized at Malay who returned her look with eager interest.

'Malay, this is Taposhi, the foster daughter of Rakhal the sculptor.' Kanika Di broke the spell.

'Oh, is she? She has grown so tall.' He moved away from the threshold, 'She is gorgeous, Ma!' Then turning to her, he said, 'How are you, Taposhi? Recognize me?'

Before she could respond, she noticed that Kanika Di was trying desperately to dispel the magic. 'Go on, Taposhi, clean the floor. You have spilled all the turmeric on Malay's clothes. Malay, go and change your clothes.' Her words brought Tapasi back to herself and effectively cut short Malay's pleasure in looking at her.

Tapasi was quite taken aback by the sensations she had felt when the young man had looked at her. Like a fragrant breeze blowing from a valley of flowers, scattering their seeds of beauty wherever they went. She had never seen a face like his. A most handsome person with such a serene face, it created ripples deep within her inner world of dreams.

However, Kanika Di's arrogance and pride, and the presence of Malay's European wife soon dispelled Tapasi's dreamworld. For the first time in her life she wanted to weep and cry loud enough for the whole world to sit up and be moved by her plight. Mercifully, she was the only one who knew of her faint and hopeless longing. An ocean can be an ocean without waves, but waves have no identity except in relation to the ocean. The ocean had no part to play in the subtle awakening of the longing in Tapasi's heart. The waves rose and fell on the surface of the sea. They came into being only to recede and perish. Tapasi felt a sense of loss even though she had no idea what she had lost. However, one thing became clear to her as she went about serving dinner, clearing the table and washing up afterwards, and that was the realization that she was nothing more than a servant there. Her identity as a schoolgirl, an intelligent person who could follow discussions in Jatin Da's drawing room, meant nothing. She was like Bholanath to them.

She would never be able to leap over the formidable 'civilized' wall surrounding Kanika Di's world. And Malay? He and his vivacious European wife circulated among the guests shaking hands with everyone, making such a handsome couplc. Dressed in her faded sari and carrying away the dirty dishes, Tapasi was excluded from their charmed circle and consigned to the dark and lonely world which society had earmarked for people like her. She was out of their periphery of vision. For the first time she was made aware of her position, of her being a perfect non-entity, of the insignificance of her life, and of Rakhal Kaka's non-existent social status.

Tapasi realized that she had been living her life in bits and pieces that didn't add up. Studying at school, cooking at home, getting thrashed by Kaka, and rushing to Kanika Di in the hope of learning something new. Circumstances had now dragged and deposited her into an obscure corner of this house where she had finally been clearly shown her place.

She stopped working abruptly and rushed home without eating anything. When she reached home, she stepped onto the veranda from where she caught a glimpse of another drama unfolding through the open door of the room. Rakhal was totally absorbed in the nude body of a woman. Snatches of conversation reached her. Tapasi turned her back on them and sat down at the far end of the veranda. She noticed that the straw mat and the bamboo curtain had been blown off her bullock-cart by a duststorm. In the dusk and the drizzle, the bullock-cart looked bare, like the unclad woman inside the room.

◆◆◆

After a couple of days, Bholanath came to fetch Tapasi. When she reached Jatin Da's house, she found Kanika Di sitting with a pretty sari in her hands. 'Taposhi, you left without a word that day! Bholanath told me you didn't eat anything. Your Jatin Da has been asking after you. And look, I have kept this sari for you. It is a gift to celebrate Malay's marriage. Here, take it and put it on. Malay's bride does not wear saris. How I wish she would. Now, go and put it on.' She spoke in her old affectionate way.

Tapasi was in no position to resist or refuse the gift. She accepted the sari quietly. Her sombre eyes searched all over for Malay, but the house was strangely silent. Just then, Jatin Da entered holding a sheet of paper. 'There's a fax from

Malay. They have reached safe and sound.'

Tapasi was about to leave when a suddenly sentimental Kanika Di wiped her eyes with the pallu of her sari and said, 'You too have grown up now, Taposhi. You should also get married. Your Rakhal Kaka tells us that Majumdar Moshai has asked for your hand.' Tapasi was stunned and realized at once that she would have to defend her position herself.

'But I want to study further, Kanika Di. I still have to finish school. I still have to take my exams. And how about my dream to study at Vishwa Bharti? Please let me study, Kanika Di! You are the only one who understands me. You are my anchor, my support. Please save me. Kaka would never say no to you. Please Didi, I don't want to get married.'

Kanika Di reasoned with her. 'Look, Taposhi, try to understand your circumstances. The history of your birth, your mother sitting in Sonagachhi, her disgrace, and Rakhal's own character. This world is nothing but a marketplace where everything changes hands. Please try to understand. A decent man with lots of money would give a name to you and a direction to your life. He'll give you a solid identity. You should accept it with reverence. It is the duty of us women to follow this path. If you resist it, your Kaka will abandon you to Sonagachhi the way he did his sister.'

'What is Sonagachhi, Didi?'

'I knew you would ask me that, Taposhi. Sonagachhi is a place in Kolkata where women who sell their bodies live. Any woman who steps in there is instantly caught in a circle of gloom from which it is impossible to come out. You have no alternative, Taposhi. Get married—that is the best thing for you.'

Suddenly Tapasi was being forced to confront another reality. She tried to make sense of her situation and to understand why it was important to get married. She pondered the fact that Kanika Di had wept when she'd learnt of Malay's marriage to the European woman, and yet, she was stressing the importance of marriage and pushing her into it. Why could not she, Taposhi, remain unmarried and pursue her studies like Maki Kazumi?

She made a last ditch effort to save herself, 'But my studies, Kanika Di? How about my dream to go to Vishwa Bharti?'

'You are so naive, Taposhi! Don't you know that women have no right to dream in our society? It is high time you stopped dreaming. You have studied enough and acquired knowledge. Is not that enough for you?'

'It is not enough for me! It is not!' Each cell of Tapasi's body reverberated in protest but there was nobody to see and share her deep anguish. Jatin Da reasoned with her in his own way. 'Taposhi, marriage will be a metamorphosis for you. Look, you'll acquire a status in society. You'll be recognized as Mrs Taposhi Majumdar.'

Tapasi returned home pale as a shadow in the water,

which shakes and shudders with every ripple. She wanted to sit quietly under the banyan tree and reflect upon her fate. Why was her future so bleak, so inundated with unspecified gloom? The feeling haunted her sleep and seemed to bind her in invisible fetters all night.

Next morning, serving tea and breakfast to Kaka, Tapasi began to wonder if there was any link at all between Rakhal the person and Rakhal the sculptor? How was she related to Kaka, who only knew how to thrash her, and who had sent her mother to Sonagachhi? He had talked to her about fear once and now he was going to marry her off. Tapasi was witness to the fact that Kaka was hopelessly addicted to toddy. He had never lived his life according to rules, ethics or social conventions. So how come he was so anxious to see her married? Had Jatin Da suggested it? Was it Majumdar's intense gaze? Money changing hands? Everything seemed to swirl around her like smoke in the room. What did it all mean?

Kaka was arranging his newly-procured bottles of toddy in a large niche in the wall. Toddy was his only addiction and he indulged in it openly. The sour smell of toddy pervaded the air and hung outside the house like mist. It was witness to all the good and bad things that took place inside the room. Tapasi wondered if her mother had also been addicted to toddy. Could that be the reason behind her deplorable plight? The stink of toddy suffocated Tapasi and made her head spin. This woman called mother—what was she like? The dim, unfamiliar face, which once she had exclusive rights on, was now lost in the anonymous darkness of sin. Suddenly, the feeling of devotion and faith she had experienced as she had gazed upon the glowing face of Tara Ma, began to diminish. Couldn't Tara Ma have performed a miracle for her? Couldn't she have met her mother just once?

A saddened Tapasi found herself at a juncture where enthusiasm, aspirations and desires were all frustrated and she was being compelled to accept marriage as her dharma. Marriage was the only way out of a desperate situation. At some level she accepted that if Nature had determined a certain path for her, it was in her own interest to follow it.

REFLECTING ON THE new misery that the future held in store for her, the distrust in Tapasi's mind deepened like the steadily intensifying darkness of the night, growing thicker and more impenetrable by the wee hours of the morning. Her trust in life, her trust in Kanika Di had crumbled.

Reaching school later in the morning, she heard of Teacher Didi's sudden death. She was shocked and intensely grieved by the news. All the girls went to Teacher Didi's house. Holding her friend's hand tight, Tapasi went too. Teacher Didi's house was in a small settlement where a handful of decrepit English and Anglo-Indian families lived. Perhaps the British government had forgotten to repatriate them or perhaps they had actually chosen to stay back in India after independence. Some of these mixed-blood families referred to England as their country and hoped to 'return' there some time. Most of them were teachers, nurses and other middle-class professionals. Teacher Didi was born in that area and now she had died there too, of some mysterious illness.

The mourners marched slowly from the house to the cemetery where Teacher Didi's body lay in a wooden casket. A couple of people were digging the ground for a grave. Wherever they dug, they found soft, muddy soil or the bones of another person already buried there. Tapasi's friend clutched her hand and said, 'The dead reside here. Also ghosts.'

'What is a ghost?'

'Oh, you don't know even that! Ghosts are fearsome beings. They have huge eyes, big ears and big teeth.' She pulled a hideous face and continued, 'And they cling to the bodies of people who happen to pass by. They suck their blood.'

A tall man dressed in a black gown arrived holding a small crucifix in his hands. Tapasi whispered, 'Who is he? Is he a...?'

'No, no, he is not a ghost. He is Padre Baba. He presides over the service in the big church situated in the middle of the basti.'

'How come I saw no priests like him in Ma's temple?'

Her friend answered, 'These people are Christians. They do not believe in Ma. They believe in Jesus Christ. And what you see over here are the graves of Christians. This place is called a cemetery.'

The friend moved ahead quickly. Tapasi looked at the rows of numberless graves where British rulers and fighters of the Indian army lay side by side.

The man in the black robe conducted the funeral. He led the prayers and all the mourners murmured the words along with him. Then he kissed the large cross he wore on a chain around his neck and the schoolgirls placed the flower garlands they had brought with them on the casket. The casket was lowered into the grave. A few mourners picked up some loose soil and covered the grave with it. The wet earth seemed to swallow everything and the ground was levelled in an instant. Teacher Didi had descended wordlessly into the underworld, to a state of non-being, like the innumerable human skeletons buried there.

Tapasi crept behind the other girls who moved like ants making their way back to school. She noticed seedlings sprouting from the cracks in the moss-covered graves. Tall grass grew here and there. Some wild flowers peeked from the vegetation in some places. Still the graveyard was a melancholy place. Tapasi walked on thinking that the desolation of the graveyard reflected her own state of mind. She wondered what the students in her class would do without Teacher Didi. Who would teach them? Would Teacher Didi turn into a skeleton under all that soil? Would she look like the one hung on the wall in the school laboratory?

Tapasi was deeply grieved by the sudden demise of her teacher. There had been just three people to guide her in this world of which she knew so little: Kanika Di, Jatin Da and Teacher Didi. Now she felt like a lost soul wandering alone in a world where nobody responded to the crying needs of her mind. What was she going to do?

By the time she returned home the shadows had lengthened in the veranda of the house and the sky was turning a deep inky blue. Kaka was not at home. Taking her schoolbooks and her blue notebook, Tapasi crept silently into bed. After a while she sat up and opened one of the books in her hand. And there, on the first page, was Tagore's translation of Kabir's famous couplet, written in Teacher Didi's beautiful hand, the letters gleaming like pearls:

Look upon life and death
There is no separation between them
The right hand and the left hand are the same.

Tapasi could not quite understand the verse. She lifted both her hands and looked at them. Are life and death like our two hands? I am living and Teacher Didi is dead. Surely there is a difference between the two?

Tapasi fell asleep eventually but half-formed, inconclusive dreams disturbed her sleep for several nights to come.

THE SUN SHONE as bright as usual in the courtyard of Tapasi's house as Kanika Didi walked down the partially-paved ground with measured steps, accompanied by a small procession of people—Bholanath, his wife and a couple of neighbours. It was a scene totally out of place in a house unused to voices, bustle or celebration of any kind. Tapasi was flustered. Suspicion filled her mind like mist. She wondered what had brought Kanika Di to the bare courtyard of a house where nothing ever happened.

The women clustered together under the banyan tree. For a fleeting moment, Tapasi played with the fanciful idea that the characters from her dreamworld had suddenly descended upon earth, though of course they weren't so worldly. The rustling leaves played accompaniment to the sound of Kanika Di's voice, much like the sound of cymbals or ankle bells accompanying a Baul song.

The women set down the goods they were carrying with them. They found a charpoy inside the house and placed it in the courtyard. Bholanath arranged the bundles and packages they had brought with them on it. Tapasi wondered what was happening. She was quite bewildered by the goings on and began to feel like an intruder in her own space.

Kanika Di stepped forward and took Tapasi's hand.

She made her sit on a mat rolled out on the floor and said, 'Come, sit here, Taposhi.' We feel no fear with those whom we love and Tapasi had no concept of what fear was. She was quite unaware of the significance of that moment in her life. At length, Kanika Di spoke up, 'The time of your *lagna* has come, Taposhi...It is the day eagerly awaited by every woman. Your Jatin Da said that Taposhi's wedding should be celebrated with proper ceremonies. Giving you away would enable us to have the privilege of *Kanyadaan*.'

Giving her away? A privilege to them? She was already detached, and far away.

Rakhal Kaka, who had been watching the scene in bewilderment, was shooed away by the women and sent off for a bath. Then they took out a sari with a red border from among the articles they had brought with them and handed it to Tapasi. 'Here, take this and put it on. Majumdar Babu's manager is expected any moment.'

Tapasi turned into an automaton and followed Kanika Di's instructions mechanically. She had never refused her. She changed into the new sari and sat down on the mat. A woman brought *dadhimangal* consisting of the tail of a fish, puffed rice and sweets, which she was fed. Presently, a little boy came running excitedly into the house shouting, 'Look, look, the *gaiholood* has come!' Two women, wives of barbers, followed, carrying gifts in covered round trays and placed them on the mat near Tapasi. All the women were curious to see what was in them. When the covers were removed they found a huge rohu fish in one tray, betelnuts, sweets and a bowlful of turmeric paste in the next and a red silk sari with golden embroidery in a plastic bag. Tapasi had never seen such a gorgeous sari before. She touched it wondering whether it was a sari or silk woven with dreams.

'Isn't it beautiful? Majumdar Babu has sent an excellent *tatva*. Our Taposhi will live like a queen. Look, he has also sent gold ornaments!' All the women busied themselves admiring the gifts and estimating their worth. 'It is only natural that he should send such expensive gifts. He has a thriving business in coal and firewood.'

Snatches of the women's talk reached Tapasi's ears. The huge rohu in the big circular tray and the opulent finery on Tapasi's body were testimony to Majumdar Babu's prosperity, but the fixed gaze of the dead fish sent a cold shiver through her body.

Rakhal Kaka brought four banana trees, which were pushed into the four corners of the square earmarked for the wedding ceremony. The women applied the *gaiholood*, the turmeric paste, on Tapasi's body after which she was given a bath. It was evening by the time the rituals were complete. All the women including Kanika Di bustled around animatedly. Tapasi was asked to change out of the red-bordered sari and the beautiful new silk sari was draped around her. The women looked at her in admiration.

'O Ma! How beautiful she looks! Like a lotus in full bloom! Where did that crazy Rakhal find this nugget of gold!'

Then someone said, 'But haven't you been rewarded handsomely for all this gold, Kanika Di? Isn't that why you are marrying her off to that Majumdar?' Tapasi was intrigued by the comment. Somebody had made a connection. Kanika Di coughed to warn the woman to shut up but Tapasi noticed the way she winked and sniggered when she'd said that Majumdar. How much she had loved and revered Kanika Di. How much she had trusted her and admired her lofty ideals. And now here she was committing Tapasi to an unholy alliance for money. Tapasi wondered whether she knew the real Kanika Di at all. She recalled how Kanika Di had prostrated herself in front of Ma at Tara Peeth. An educated person does not worship Ma in that manner and yet she had. A person like Kanika Di, the wife of a scholar like Jatin Da, had done *ulat* darshan of Ma!

Dressed in a dhoti-kurta and sporting a sandalwood paste tilak on his forehead, the priest was busy making preparations for the wedding. Once the ceremony was in full swing, he was like a juggler, picking up leaves, pouring water into the vessels and muttering mantras under his breath. At length, he called Tapasi to come and perform the *moochi bhagna* ceremony. She had to smash four unbaked clay pots full of water, one each placed under the four banana trees, with the big toe of her right foot. She broke them one by one, as instructed by the priest. The people around her were enjoying themselves. There was much laughter and lively conversation. They were eating sweets. She was the only one fasting since morning. A woman snickered in her ear, 'Your days of virginity are over, Taposhi.' Tapasi's instant impulse was to ask, 'What is virginity' But it was imperative to keep quiet at that moment.

Soon they saw a cloud of dust in the distance and the notes from a small trumpet floated in on the wind. The children from the neighbourhood clapped and said excitedly, '*Barjaatri* is coming, *barjaatri* is coming!' And Kanika Di and her companions rushed to the entrance of the house, while Rakhal followed diffidently. Soon two women entered the threshold with Majumdar Babu dressed in a spotless white dhoti-kurta and cap. They were followed by Jatin Da and sundry other folk. Tapasi looked wide-eyed at the newcomers. She noticed that the bridegroom was almost Jatin Da's age. Was this man her soon-to-be husband? Or was he the embodiment of a hideous deceit?

The wedding guests busied themselves eating sweets and drinking sherbet. Tapasi looked anxiously at her broken bullock-cart. She thought she saw someone trying to hide behind it. A woman—because she noticed the pallu of a printed sari caught in the straw screen fluttering like a flag in the dusky breeze of late evening. Tapasi longed to rise from her place and run to the bullock-cart for a better view of the woman but she was prevented from doing so by the wedding rituals—*saptpadi* with *shaligram* as a witness, mantras, the edge of her sari tied in a knot with another cloth, the voice of the priest, other voices ululating, aromatic rings of rising smoke, unknown hands lifting the stool on which she was sitting with betel leaves covering her eyes. Tapasi was like a character performing a role in a play. Covering her head with the *lajja vastra*, the raiment of honour, Majumdar Babu filled the parting in her hair with vermilion powder sprinkled through his gold ring. The vermilion shone bright on her broad forehead and heavy long hair. Transforming her from a non-entity, a *shankha paula*, the emblem of the auspicious state of wifehood, was slipped on her slender wrist. A faint whisper, somehow not so joyous, was doing the rounds, 'The marriage is solemnized.'

The bustle and noise outside subsided slowly. Everybody left. Tapasi had heard that she would be sent away the next day. A tired Tapasi took off the red silk sari, changed into her old one, and lay down quietly on her mat.

◆◆◆

The night following the wedding ceremony—her last night in that room—Tapasi got up suddenly, feeling flustered. She'd dreamt of a woman. Two pale, feeble hands caressing her forehead, a few indistinct words of affection, of a kind she had never heard before and which now she could not properly recall. Drops of water falling on her forehead—but she had seen no eyes so they could not be tears. A certain touch. Words. Tears. A faceless, nameless, presence.

But who was the woman? The one who lay close to her and who vanished before dawn? Tapasi found a small packet wrapped in cloth lying on the mat. It was proof that the stranger had visited her last night. She found a gold bangle in the packet. A strange tenderness filled Tapasi's heart as she slipped the kangan onto her slender wrist. She had never felt such warmth before. Was marriage like the warmth of the body of the mysterious woman who had lain close to her last night?

The morning breeze slowly filled the room. Tapasi bathed hurriedly and put on her red silk sari. The time of leave-taking—*suryapranam* and *vidai*, was upon them. Majumdar Babu had come alone to take her away. Kanika Di, Jatin Da, and the women from the neighbourhood were conspicuous by their absence. Rakhal bid her a mute farewell and sent her away with nothing substantial. There were new clothes in a bundle and the bangle on her wrist. As she boarded Majumdar Babu's vehicle, she heard Rakhal's door close behind her. Tapasi wondered why the bright patch of sun, which accompanied her to school everyday, remained frozen far behind.

◆◆◆

Boarding Majumdar Babu's old car was a novel experience. He sat very close to her but spoke no words to her all the way. Within an hour or two Tapasi, gazing out of the car's glass window, saw all the familiar sights recede. Her locality, the unpaved road, then the buildings of Vishwa Bharti with the Chhatim Tila hidden behind them, Didi's tea-stall across the road. The bumpy drive unleashed a host of memories unhinging them in her mind, sending them crashing into smithereens inside her.

'Come, get off the car,' Majumdar Babu opened the door for her and laughed. Tapasi shivered at the sight of his yellow teeth set in black gums.

Getting off the car she saw a small brick house with a sandstone platform. A few flower pots with large and small plants were arranged on either side. The entrance to the house was on the other end of the platform. Tapasi walked slowly towards the entrance. She saw an elderly woman filling a large brass basin with milky water. Majumdar Babu, who had been leading Tapasi towards the entrance, stepped aside and laughed self-consciously. The woman said, 'Come, come. Dip your feet in this basin before you enter the house. I don't know how to conduct *boi baran...*' She grinned toothlessly and then, as if hit by a bolt of lightning exclaimed, 'O Ma, the bride is the Goddess incarnate!' Her smile faded into a profound silence. A secret apprehension seemed to have taken hold of her.

Inside, the house was shabby and unkempt. Unwashed clothes, dirty dishes, torn paper and other rubbish lay about all over the house. After offering her a chair, Majumdar disappeared. The old woman brought Tapasi a glass of water and said, 'It is good that you have come, Boi. Now you should take over your household. I have grown old and my vision is bad.'

'Are you his mother?' Tapasi asked spontaneously.

'No, I am not,' she burst out laughing, 'I am his Dai Ma. His family has deserted him. I brought him up and helped him set up his business. Naren is like my son. I've been after him to get married for long. So finally he agreed. He must have suddenly thought who would cook for him once Dai Ma dies!' She chuckled. A feeble cough and a wheezing attack followed. Tapasi got off the chair and helped her lie down.

Night descended into the room through the windows. Dai Ma got up and served Tapasi daal and bhat, which she ate quietly. After she finished, Dai Ma took away the dishes to the kitchen, which was at the other end of the house. There she unrolled a straw mat on the floor and exhausted by her continuous cough, lay down to sleep. Tapasi rested her head against a wall and leaned against it, her mind blank. Her eyes rested on the gold kangan scratched here and there. Each scratch seemed to her to conceal secrets of its previous owner. She was dreaming about it when she heard a voice calling out loudly, 'Have you fallen asleep?'

Tapasi was startled. As she tried to get up from the dhurrie, Majumdar Babu all but threw himself on her. A foul smell permeated the dark room. Coarse hands began to grab and pummel her body. Foul smelling teeth dug into her flesh. Her sari was ripped off. She felt his naked body squashed against hers. She tried to ward him off by holding her hands above her face but to no avail. Her body was vanquished. Tapasi was utterly helpless as Majumdar claimed the rights of a husband over her. The night seemed to stretch endlessly.

Tapasi spent the next several days in a state of perpetual exhaustion and mental inertia. She moved around, ate and drank like a puppet on a string. The days went by and she realized that certain lifestyles offered no scope for thinking and dreaming about the future. Household chores, the charge of the kitchen, all fell to her lot, as if they had been waiting for her.

Dai Ma's resistance had collapsed and she had taken to bed. Tapasi's day was spent in monotonous silence and exhausting household work. Dai Ma would cough and say a few words about her health and turn on her side. Tapasi knew nothing about Majumdar's past. All she got acquainted with was the house, the furniture, the bedclothes, the goods that the manager brought, the rice, the piles of paddy in the store, the steel cupboard, and the leaf bowls full of sweets. The food was plentiful and she ate well. At night, Majumdar Babu always brought her a glass of milk along with one for himself. She wore silk saris and slept on a soft and cozy bed. But the nights were a battleground of ceaseless wrestling, which reduced her to a state of semi-consciousness.

In the morning she was back to her normal chores. A kind of stasis had taken hold of her sensibilities. Her mind had given up its innate habit of asking questions.

The sweeperwoman was the only one who talked to her. In the beginning she only spoke of this and that. With time she became a little forward. She would look at Tapasi's face and say, 'We are created by Brahma, Vishnu preserves us and Shiva is the one who destroys. We have no control over our destiny, Boi Di.' She would look as grave as a philosopher when she uttered these words. Tapasi, who had once been able to understand everything, now responded with a silly smile and went back to her work. The work included some unusual things. She had to cook special dishes. She had to add powders and potions not familiar to her to the meat cooking in the pan. She often arranged boxes and bottles of medicines with prescriptions from vaids and hakeems in a steel cupboard. Majumdar alone consumed these special meat dishes and medicines.

One day, Tapasi had to cook the meat with a peculiar, foul-smelling, yellow substance. The revolting fumes pervaded the house. Once it was done, Tapasi transferred the meat to a serving dish and promptly rushed to the water tap where she threw up. Dai Ma crept out of her bed and came to her. She exclaimed, 'I knew I would not depart without seeing my grandson!'

The sweeperwoman stopped what she was doing, rolled her eyes meaningfully and said, 'Oh, you wretched hag! Isn't it bad enough that you brought a poor man's daughter here? And now you utter such lies through your toothless mouth! Don't you know the truth? How long can you hide it? Oh, Shiva, Shiva.'

Trembling helplessly, an exhausted Tapasi listened to the two women. The sweeperwoman turned to Tapasi and said, 'Do you know what you've just cooked, Boi Di? You've cooked meat with crocodile's semen. God knows from where he procures such things. But has anybody ever benefited by eating them? That bastard is an actor and you are so naive.'

'Who is an actor?' Tapasi asked wide-eyed.

'You are too simple, Boi Di. You are so young. A poor man's child. What sort of people are your father and brothers to sell you to this man? They have flung you into a living hell! You are paying for their sins. Doesn't he beat you up afterwards? He is sure to. He is bound to thrash you or else how would he give vent to his frustrated lust?'

The conversation ended abruptly with a knock on the door. The fat man who sold groceries entered the house. He handed Tapasi some daal, rice, salt, oil and a bottle of some colourful potion. Then he smirked, 'This is Majumdar Moshai's medicine. Keep it carefully.'

The grocer's eyes were bloodshot and his words heavy with veiled meaning. He guffawed and the sweeperwoman laughed insolently. The sound of their laughter was like rocks thrown at a wall. Such a frightening din. Slowly, understanding dawned on her, layer by layer. Her confusion seemed to get dispelled at last.

But the very same night, after a bout of coughing, Dai Ma breathed her last. There were no tears, pity or compassion for her in Majumdar's eyes. Only Tapasi looked stricken as she moved about timidly, not knowing what to do. An undertaker took away the body. Dai Ma's dhurrie, bedsheets and bundle of clothes were sent to a *dom*. The corner of the house where Dai Ma died was cleaned up and Tapasi and the sweeperwoman lit some incense sticks and placed them there. It was ironical that the sweeperwoman, who took the rubbish away from the house, was instructing Tapasi in the ways of spirituality. Still Tapasi felt terribly lonely in that brick and mortar structure she called home. Maybe her questioning persona was coming to the fore all over again. The people in Jatin Da's house and their conversations, assemblies, school, studies, Teacher Didi's death...so many things had slipped away from her.

◆◆◆

Tapasi was fighting a losing battle in her so-called home. Majumdar's potion-swilling habits overpowered her. She soon realized that the glass of milk Majumdar brought her every night was laced with some pink substance. This was followed by a grapple of bodies during which she felt as if she had been flung into a spiky ditch. Then a frustrated Majumdar thrashed her mercilessly to prove himself victorious. He was the husband. It was his birthright to be the winner. By morning, Tapasi would recover from the influence of the pink substance mixed with the milk in her glass. Recalling the events of the night before and with her bruised and battered body, she attended to household work as if nothing had happened. Her scepticism, her enquiring mind, no longer cooperated with her.

Majumdar was the one who did all the talking in the house. He talked, ordered and abused her. Even when he was away his presence pervaded the house like stale, putrid air. His word was absolute law and the speech locked within Tapasi's lips was stilled forever. Her status in the house was that of a slave—Some mysteries were never unravelled, but some became clearer....

Every now and then he would mention the big money he had paid Jatin Da for her hand as well as the large sum that Rakhal had drunk away. Mute and helpless, she was bound to be sold. Bargaining was the culture of the market. She had been pushed into this mire by so many middlemen and agents. She felt cynical and devoid of faith. A deep bitterness ran through Tapasi's veins. She had had a strong, unconditional trust in Jatin Da. Mesmerized by his words, she had dreamed of a new world of promise for herself. But when the mist cleared she found herself in a place where the answers to all her doubts were harsh and bitter. The only person who empathized with her was the sweeperwoman. She comforted and reassured her and encouraged her to be strong.

Every now and then Majumdar's friends and relatives would come visiting. Struggling with perpetual fatigue, Tapasi cooked and served food to them. They called her bhabi, brother's wife, but she barely registered their faces in her mind. The only faces that had left a lasting imprint on her mind were those of the people who had thronged Jatin Da's house and Didi's tea-stall. There was one single wish engraved on her own mind—to study at the university and to learn what lay ahead of her. But even that small wish had been clamped shut like Teacher Didi's body in a casket and buried under Majumdar's ceaseless atrocities. The house was like a graveyard, devoid of the will to live. She remembered what her friend had once told her. That nobody flounders after death. She too did not flounder. She was surrounded in a situational vacuum where cuts and bruises covered her body but she endured the violence with clenched teeth. No groans or sobs escaped her mouth. All she responded with, was silence.

◆◆◆

Tapasi found pleasure and respite in taking care of the potted plants outside the house. She tended and watered them and cheered up seeing them in bloom. Looking at the flowers, she would forget the pain of the bruises and welts that Majumdar's cane had left on her limbs. Often in the mornings, the sweeperwoman would cluck in sympathy and say, 'How long can you put up with this? How much courage can you have? Why are you putting up with it, Boi Di? Don't you have any other place to go?'

Tapasi felt that a whole lot of lines were emerging on her forehead. Lines, which spread and stretched, pulling and dragging her far, far away.

Tapasi had not eaten anything all day and had refused her customary glass of milk at night. She felt her head begin to clear—as if the dusty cobwebs in her head had been removed and words had at last begun to form on her chapped lips. When Majumdar assaulted her that night she abruptly disentangled herself from his clutches, sprang up and stood apart. Rolling her eyes like the sweeperwoman, she began to scream, 'Enough now! Don't touch me. I have had enough of you. I can take it no more. If you so much as touch me again, I'll kill you. I'll not spare you. Who do you think I am?'

She twisted her long, loose hair into a knot and felt as if she was returning to herself. Majumdar was stunned. His eyes were wide open, his body shook like an autumn leaf and the hand which he had raised to beat her with was frozen in the air. The foul-smelling mouth which uttered abuses, hung open in astonishment. The musty half darkness of the room had grown more acrid. Like a vanquished demon the astounded monster cowed down. Tapasi realized that the 'fear' with which she had entered the house had slipped from her body like a sheet and now covered Naren Majumdar's body.

All of a sudden her husband shuddered and turned his face away. Tapasi, who had freed herself from that bed of tyranny after such a long time, slept by herself, fully clothed, on a straw mat on the floor.

In the morning, Majumdar flitted around the house like a spectre in a cremation ground looking disgruntled and unnerved. When Tapasi placed tea and breakfast on a teapoy for him as usual, he attacked the food as always but anger scorched his body like an electric current. As soon as he finished eating, he raised the empty breakfast thaali over his head and assaulted Tapasi with it.

'You dared to answer me back. Me? I am your husband. I've spent thousands of rupees on you. What haven't I given you? A house, clothes, jewels... an identity! And you, a harlot's offspring, you raised your voice in front of me! What is your worth, anyway? You say you'll hit me. Come, hit me. I'll see how you do that.' He began to thrash her with the thaali, an umbrella, shoes and whatever else he could lay his hands on. Tapasi almost fainted from the impact of his blows. With blood streaming down her forehead and dizziness overpowering her, she gathered her courage somehow and declared, 'I'll kill you. I'll not spare you!'

'You'll kill me. Me? Do you realize that you'll be a widow when I am dead? You'll not get even boiled rice and raw bananas after my death. And, in case you have designs on my business and property, then let it be known to you, Taposhi, that my cousin is not going to give you a penny!'

But Tapasi had fainted before he could finish his speech. She lay bloodied and unconscious for quite some time. Her physical and mental faculties had failed her that night. In the morning the sweeperwoman came and woke her up. She offered her water to drink and then tried to make her see reason. 'You'll perish one day. He is neither going to mend his ways nor is he going to be a man. That is a nasty gash on your head. Come, I'll take you to a doctor.'

All landscapes of the external world seemed to have vanished from Tapasi's eyes. Their outlines had faded from her soul. In her benumbed state of mind it was as if she had even forgotten how to walk. There was so much outside the house. Roads, crossroads, pathways, fresh air, the emerald green mantle of Nature... She was stepping out of the house after nearly two years. Holding the sweeperwoman's hand and sitting in a rickshaw, she seemed to be moving in a state of oblivion, a castaway hoping to glimpse the shore of an island.

◆◆◆

The doctor cleaned the wound, dressed and bandaged it. He asked her questions in a soothing, velvety voice. His words were like a balm to her wounded sensibility. They restored her self-awareness. She was being revitalized. It was imperative that she took a decision and adhered to it but a half-conscious person cannot take decisions. She had to learn a lot of things. But does a promise made to oneself ever help? The memories no longer swelled like a tide. The sweeperwoman's words were too basic. How should she go about taking a decision?

Majumdar returned home completely sozzled that night and flopped onto his bed never to leave it again. The next few days were spent in a haze of doctor's visits, medical tests, medicines hoarded in the cupboard, potions simmering in the kadhai, their reactions, the pain behind the groans. Tapasi had only now begun to understand the kind of man she had been living with. The shocked look in the doctor's eyes made her realize the truth, discovering which she felt utterly mortified. It was humiliating to know that God had not even created an ordinary man for her, though the world teemed with millions of normal people. What a mockery of her existence! Her first impulse was to run away somewhere and end her life. But Majumdar's deteriorating health forced her to stay. So she gave him medicines, soothed his brow and massaged the hands that had thrashed her.

Tapasi found the doctor's visits a big relief. He came, gave the medicine and spent some time with the patient. He was dignified and compassionate. He brought medicines not only for Majumdar but for Tapasi too. 'You need to take this medicine, Taposhiji. You've been drugged and tortured so much that your blood pressure has gone up alarmingly. You should eat properly. And take care of yourself.'

The doctor came and went everyday. Tapasi looked after Majumdar and also took medicines herself. Slowly she began to feel normal again, as if she was climbing back out after falling into an abyss. The giddiness, insomnia and fuzzy emptiness inside her slowly began to clear but Majumdar was growing sicker by the day. In spite of medical treatment and her unstinting care he showed no signs of improvement. His business manager would visit from time to time to hand over cash to Tapasi for day-to-day requirements.

The storm seemed to have been lulled for a while and life was falling into a regular pattern. A bit of peace had descended on the household. However, it proved to be just a brief interlude for then Naren Majumdar's cousin, Ramdas, landed up from Kolkata greatly agitated. He quickly assumed charge of the house—appropriating the keys, the money and the documents from the safe. Tapasi tried to protect herself from Ramdas's gaze, which followed her everywhere. Drawing water from the well, cooking food in the kitchen or feeding the patient, she could feel his eyes bore into her back. She became a virtual prisoner in the kitchen. Ramdas put a clamp on the doctor's visits, medicines and injections. As a result, the marginal improvement in Majumdar's health was nullified and his condition began rapidly to deteriorate. There were others who had followed Ramdas. The ailing Majumdar was thronged by relatives all claiming a special place in his heart and Tapasi figured nowhere. She was excluded from his list of relatives despite the sindoor he had put in the parting in her hair.

When Naren Majumdar groaned with pain through the night Tapasi would rush to give him sips of water and milk. She soothed and massaged his aching limbs with the fast depleting supply of oil in the house while he watched her mutely with eyes brimming with tears. His words and their harshness were sealed inside his mouth. A change had come over the house. Now Ramdas's word was law. Everybody obeyed him.

Majumdar's journey of pain lasted for a few months. One morning as she entered the room with tea and breakfast, she was appalled to find his frail, lifeless body lying on the floor beside his bed, his wide-open eyes staring at the ceiling. By the time a flustered Tapasi could attend to him, Ramdas materialized from a corner of the room and began to scream at her, 'Don't touch my brother! Don't desecrate his body! Ever since you set foot in this house he became ill.' Tapasi stood helplessly by as he heaped abuses and levelled all sorts of allegations at her. Instead of tears, a vast desert of sand settled into Tapasi's eyes.

People began to pour into the house. More and more

relatives crowded around talking about their special bond with the deceased and pretending to mourn his passing though their eyes remained dry. Someone led Tapasi to the bank of the river and smashed her *shankha paula* with a grindstone. Back home, she was left sitting alone in a corner of the house. Someone fetched a plain, borderless sari for her to wear. She was given only one meal of raw banana, sago and unboiled milk a day. No fish, lentils or rice were served to her. Once or twice the sweeperwoman sneaked in a small basket containing roasted puffed rice which Tapasi would eat stealthily in a house crawling with men and women.

It was ironical. All those days when she had been struggling against injustice, nobody came to the house. And now, when everything was over, countless relatives had gathered around. Yet, not one of them identified with her or was concerned that she had been Majumdar's legally wedded wife. They followed their own agenda. They arrived and left at their convenience. The sweeperwoman tried to enlighten Tapasi. 'They are busy selling off Majumdar Babu's belongings and raking in money. Soon his land and business assets will be put on sale. Even the house will go.'

"What is to become of me, Tapasi Majumdar?" Tapasi wondered. What does the future hold for me? Sitting in her widow weeds in a corner, she was affixing her signature on various documents, wherever she was asked. Tapasi was nothing. She was a non-entity. Am I invisible? How come nobody notices my existence? Why is it so?

She waited for a new dawn but the sun simply refused to rise for her.

◆◆◆

Majumdar's body lay on a pyre in the cremation ground. A small crowd of relatives stood around. Suddenly, Tapasi caught a glimpse of a familiar face amongst them. She searched her memory and discovered that the face belonged to Rakhal Kaka. How come he had landed up here? A woman with her head covered with the pallu of her sari stood by him. Who was she? Was she a real woman or a shadow? Though she stared intently at the woman Tapasi could not identify her. Who was she? Tapasi's memory yielded no outlines of her face. Kanika Di? No, no, couldn't be Kanika Di.

Tapasi was dragged to a platform and made to sit there to get her head tonsured. A barber approached. Tapasi was now completely dazed by the happenings of the last few days. All eyes were fixed on her when suddenly they swivelled their gaze onto the mystery woman loudly screaming, 'Let go of her. Let go! Don't cut her hair!'

Her powerful voice stunned the spectators. The barber's hands froze. No one dared challenge the unknown, unfamiliar stranger. Tapasi rose from her place, her eyes full of astonishment. Who was the woman who raised her voice for her? She saw Rakhal Kaka spring into action and grab the woman's hand. The sweeperwoman tried to free the woman from his hold, but couldn't and the woman hastily handed her a bundle before being swallowed by the crowd.

When they reached home, the sweeperwoman gave Tapasi the bundle. Tapasi untied it and found two used saris, two silver ornaments, and some money. But what amazed her was a gold bangle exactly like the one left by her side on the night of the day she was married, the one with a few dents and scratches. The kangans made a connection and told a story about an obscure part of Tapasi's life, which she was unable to understand. What she understood, however, was that there was something hugely significant about that treasure. So she wrapped it up in the edge of her sari and secured it closely around her waist. Who was she? 'Prashna' Tapasi was ready to take over.

Part III

THE SUN HAD only just spun its web of light but the first hint of its warmth had already woken the wretched inmates of the bleak ashram at the bottom of the road. They all—Vrinda, Noorabai, Bhagwati, were driven by only one force. Hunger. The hunger of a rumbling, empty stomach. Hunger was the problem they faced night and day. From the moment they awoke, till the time they fell asleep, hunger dominated their routine. Those who roam the wilderness see only mirages. The fire in their bellies drives them round and round and makes them dance to its tune.

Tapasi had become tired of wandering. Has one ever caught a mirage by drifting among them? Her perpetual hunger and thirst, the jaap in the temple, the meaninglessly formidable life of the ashram—she had defied them all by leaving the temple abruptly for a few days. And now Ambika Devi was teaching her a lesson. She had her beaten up mercilessly. She was given no food for three days. Madam had sneaked her a little milk and a fruit one night. What sort of a life was this? She was alive still, in spite of the beating and humiliation. And yet, there were no tears in her eyes. Ambika Devi had put Tapasi's palms under the legs of her chair and then lowered her bulk onto it, sitting that way for several hours till Tapasi fell unconscious. The others quietly took in the congealed blood on her hands and the bruises and welts on her body. At night they fed her scraps saved from their rotis, gave her water to drink and helped her take a bath. Madam bought an ointment from the market and applied it gently on Tapasi's wounds. But wounds do not heal so fast. Dimly, in a half stupor, Tapasi heard their voices around her.

'Why did you run away from the temple? You should let things be as they are. You know Ambika Devi, don't you? *Baba Rey...* How mercilessly she beat you! Where was the need to ask her to account for the money she had embezzled...?'

Then Barota said, 'You are educated. You should have kept quiet. Isn't it enough that this administration has protected us from prostitution?'

'Yes of course it has,' Noorabai said tearfully. 'But how can one put up with Ambika Devi's atrocities to cover up her faults?'

'She hates Tapasi's guts,' Vrinda said with a laugh, 'A liar likes other liars. And she knows Tapasi is not one.'

Listening to them talk, Tapasi recalled Majumdar's face

and the terrible reality of his inadequate body revealed to her by the sweeperwoman's shameless laughter. She had known no pleasure but the definition of pain had been amply revealed to her. Pain had been as pervasive in Bolepur as it was in Vrindavan.

◆◆◆

A few days later, when she was summoned to Ambika Devi's office, Tapasi was apprehensive—like the blind man whose sight has been restored but who still walks with his cane. It takes a lifetime to build your trust in people. She had trusted Jatin Da, Kanika Di, and Ambika Devi's social commitment, and look what she got in return. She entered the room with trepidation and raised her lowered eyes briefly to see Ambika Devi sitting resplendent, in her usual regal position, on a chair. She got up and took Tapasi's hand.

'Tapasi, meet Jaimala Devi. Jaimalaji, this is Tapasi. She is well educated. Given an opportunity she can go far.'

Tapasi was confused. She looked from Ambika Devi to the dignified lady sitting on the chair opposite her. She was middle-aged, fair and frail. Dressed in a white silk sari, her head decorously covered with her pallu, her face was as exquisite as it was serene. Her blue eyes were a little heavy with age but still so captivating that Tapasi could not interpret their expression in a rational way. She had never seen such an earnest, direct and attractive gaze. She wondered what kind of trick this was—a face illumined by a beatific smile that made a direct appeal to one's heart, like the fragrant colours of the flowers in Jatin Da's garden.

How many days and nights had she now spent in the gloom of the ashram offering jaaps without faith, in the temples? Was it one year, or five? She had lost all sense of time. Nervously, she ran the tips of her fingers on the raised blue blotches on her palms. She looked down at her own ravaged hands, discoloured from rough work. Each pore of her body ached with weariness.

'Tapasi, Jaimalaji has opened a school. She needs teachers. You are educated. Would you like to go with her?'

Tapasi's wishes had not once determined the choices that were made for her. She had no right to expect anything from her life nor draw any conclusions from her experiences. Still, she could not suppress the hope that suddenly filled her. Ambika Devi's sharp, stinging words and taunts appeared totally unreal now. An undefinable joy, like drops of water from a cool spring began to douse the fire smouldering inside her.

'Yes, I'd like to do that,' she struggled to answer in a level voice, though a storm raged inside her.

'Think it over, *beta*. It is an extremely modest venture. We have a lot of difficulties and problems but I'll be there with you. This is Nandita. And this is Uddhavji. We'll all work together.' The two people Jaimala Devi introduced came and stood beside her. Nandita had a plain face and a full figure. She wore a bindi on her forehead, sindoor in the parting of her hair and lots of glass bangles. Uddhavji was a middle-aged man in a dhoti-kurta. He wore an expression of rigid arrogance, like the face of the chief of a muth. He sported a grey moustache and beard. They talked among themselves but Tapasi barely registered what they had to say.

What does the future hold for me now? What are these people really like? Who is honest and to what extent? Am I strong enough to cope with the reality of future circumstances? What new role am I being selected to play? Her mind teemed with questions. But yes, a word, utterly sweet, resonated so deeply through her being. Someone had called her *beta*, child. How unfamiliar and yet how lovely it sounded. The word sank into her heart and nestled there —a treasure she had never known before. Though Tapasi could barely identify it, there was something in that voice, something in the personality of that graceful woman, which encouraged her. A pair of blue eyes were beckoning her to fly the vast expanse of the sky, and for once, the sky seemed infinite to her, full of possibilities, with its depth and vastness stretching to unknown expanses.

A voice seemed to rise from the deep recesses of Tapasi's consciousness: *Manusher monchoy manusheri mon* (The human heart longs for human intimacy). Her heart had always longed for human warmth but what had she got in the bargain? Marriage, the ashram and unfulfilled dreams and desires, stirring, galling, unending desires—and finally the heart-wrenching words, 'I am there with you.'

Hugging these words close to her heart Tapasi bade farewell to the ashram. She rushed to her room and collected her scant belongings—including the blue notebook—from a dark corner. The gold kangans had been snatched off her bruised wrists by someone when she had lain semi-conscious. Barota, Noorabai, Vrinda and Mariam came to the gate to see her off. They were silent. Standing at the threshold of a new life, Tapasi felt utterly lost. She was new in the world. *Manusheri*, humanity, caste, merit, relationships—they were all hollow, disconnected words. So why did she feel such regret at parting from these dejected and depraved women—women whom the world had chosen to discard?

◆◆◆

Tapasi walked away without a single backward glance and climbed into a rickshaw with Nandita. The rickshaw forged ahead leaving behind the streets, the open drains and the piles of stinking garbage. The road, the slush and the muck she used to traverse with her companions on her way to the temple receded in the background. She bade a silent farewell to the winding streets, the dismal corners, the muths and temples where she had found no peace of mind and which had never once excited the sort of enthusiasm she had felt walking down the lush green avenues of Vishwa Bharti.

When the rickshaw approached the intersection in

front of the bank where the journalist used to give his fiery speeches, Tapasi noted how desolate the place looked without him. His words had been so thought-provoking, stirring her deeply and raising so many questions in her heart. And his body reeling under the merciless blows of the crowd, his blank face, his broken glasses, his threadbare clothes, his severed tongue, his feeble hands stretching out to beg, and his collapse from hunger, were his reward for speaking the truth. Tapasi shuddered down to her bones. She imagined the journalist becoming an extension of her own ego and pervading her consciousness. Like her, he too had put up with unspeakable suffering for the sake of truth—a truth which did not relate to any vested interest and was ethical, universal and free from personal motive. *Manusher monchoy manusheri mon...*

Vrindavan was left behind. The rickshaw pulled into a narrow street off the main road. Nandita tried to start a conversation but soon gave up on finding Tapasi lost in a world of her own, remote from her situational existence. Eventually, they reached the Kusum Sarovar. Tapasi had been there before. The minute she got off the rickshaw and stepped onto the ground she felt an affinity with the place. Her heart beat for it like it once had for Bolepur.

'Aamar eiy pai chalaar anand.
Khaley yaye—rodra dhaya varsha—aasey vasant.'
(Now that I am walking, I am exhilarated by my walk.

Nature and self-confidence keep step with me. Seasons change but I keep walking. I shall continue to walk with firm steps).

The feel of the ground of Kusum Sarovar beneath her feet and the gentle sunshine caressing the winter air, made Tapasi feel as if the frost within her was beginning to thaw. The chill was being dispelled. The warmth in the still air began to shred the time suspended within her. As if something was setting her free. The air of dejection that had engulfed her for so long began to dissipate. The face of the muted journalist and his utterances came back to her mind. Jatin Da had often used the word *alter ego*. Had the persona of the journalist become a part of her own consciousness?

◆◆◆

A class was in progress in the 'school' where about twenty children in shabby uniforms sat cross-legged on a dhurrie in a small room. Their hands and feet were filthy. A plain, bespectacled, dark-skinned teacher, her head covered with the pallu of her sari, was teaching them a song to the accompaniment of a harmonium placed on a rickety table. Her voice was melodious, quite in contrast to her not-so-attractive appearance.

Hum honge kamyab, hum honge kamyab ek din
Man mein hai vishwas, poora hai vishwas
Hum honge kamyab ek din.

The words of the song, *We Shall Overcome*, vibrant with

pristine energy surged through Tapasi's body like an electric current. It was such an energizing song! She stood against a wall and took in the scene in front of her. The school was a small, derelict place. A torn and threadbare dhurrie—dirty, puny, emaciated children with bleary eyes and runny noses—flies swarming all over them. A scene from the documentary she had seen on Sudan and Somalia flashed in her mind. It was as if those children had been transported here.

The three or four rooms that constituted the school were all furnished with desks and chairs but the children occupying them were so dirty that they looked incongruous seated at them. One room was an office of sorts. Uddhavji's son, Ghanshyam, took care of administrative chores such as the arrangements for teaching, accounts, salaries of the four teachers and sundry other things. The school was supported by the patronage of an organization in Delhi. Nandita, Gayatri and the music teacher had been appointed recently. Tapasi was to stay in the basti opposite the school where Jaimala Devi resided in a two-room unit with a kitchen and veranda on the ground floor of the house. Tapasi was given a room upstairs. She was to have her meals with Jaimala Devi. A woman servant cooked and took care of the other household chores in the morning and later helped out in the school, thus receiving her salary from there.

All the children in the school came from a colony called Nagla, which was a basti of snake charmers. Since their profession was dying out—snake shows having lost their entertainment value in the face of seductive TV programmes—the erstwhile snake charmers eked out a living as mimics and harlequins. During the melas on Rama Navami and Janamashtmi, they posed as sanyasis and accepted charity. Occasionally, they joined gangs of dacoits. The public at large, nervous about its security, avoided their habitat as a matter of course. It was with all these circumstances in mind that Nandita asked Tapasi, 'You won't feel scared about living alone in this room, Tapasi, would you? This area is crawling with thieves and disreputable characters.'

How could Tapasi tell her that the word 'fear' had left her a long time ago? She did not know what fear meant. She answered, 'I'll see, Nanditaji. Right now, after the ashram, a room to myself and all this privacy is very pleasant. To have a room of my own is sheer heaven. Besides, I am fortunate to be living close to a lady like Jaimalaji. I seem to be returning to myself at last.'

Nandita stared at her, incredulous. An ordinary Bengali widow talking so gracefully—her words sincere and full of sense; her gaze so earnest and her appearance so serene she looked as if she had just bathed in dew.

◆◆◆

Most of Tapasi's time was taken by the children in the school. Before she settled down to teaching them, she roped in the woman helper of the school and gave each child a thorough scrub. She persuaded Uddhavji to provide a few cakes of soap and called a barber in to give the children a haircut. She clipped their nails. In two or three days, the children's clothes were washed and dried. Almost overnight, a magical transformation came over the small school. A feel-good spontaneity pervaded the place. Gayatri, Nandita, Uddhav, Ghanshyam, the helper and, most of all, Jaimala Devi watching from afar—all seemed to be bonding together through intangible ties. Devotion to duty was manifest in the joyous celebration of their work. Everybody looked cheerful. The children were happy. Washed and bathed, they drank the milk provided by the school and smiled and laughed a lot. Tapasi too felt happy and laughed often though not without wondering what kind of laughter it was. Whatever kind it might be, she was sure the spontaneous, full-throated, tinkling laughter of the schoolchildren would never be described as 'uncouth' or 'uncivilized'.

◆◆◆

The Kusum Sarovar pond was surrounded by a splendid embankment adorned with turrets, viewing galleries and arched eaves—ample testimony to its artisans' talents. The great pond situated within an open courtyard despite its isolation was not a lonely place. Even though there was a layer of scum on the surface of the water, those who bathed in it were convinced of its sanctity. There was a never ending stream of visitors to the place at all times of the day. The modest school run by Jaimala Devi was adjacent to the Kusum Sarovar compound. Uddhavji's temple snuggled against its front wall and Mauni Baba's humble dwelling, with a veranda made of unfinished sandstone, was situated nearby on fallow land unadorned by pretty trees or plants of any kind save a few thorny babool trees, their slender branches and fine leaves perpetually covered with a layer of dust. They looked straggly and neglected. Kusum Sarovar was supposed to be symbolic of depth, wisdom and a gentle sensitivity capable of providing an inner vision to believers. The modest school building seemed to be standing on tiptoe, stretching its body upward and holding its hands aloft in supplication to it.

The ambience of the school seemed to have lit up the land around it. Jaimala Devi was constantly engaged in spreading light. She collected clothes and cash donations from individuals and organizations and created resources to give shape and character to the school. Tapasi was astonished to learn that Jaimala Devi had once been a film star. And now, Tapasi had strengthened the flickering flame of the light started by Jaimala Devi. Tapasi was already experiencing a change, sensing a new vigour and direction in herself. She felt free and capable. As if her life had reached another turning point and this time the road ahead did not impede her. Life was moving ahead.

The feeling when she received her first salary was indescribable. It was money earned by the sweat of her brow, the honest reward of hard work. The money glowed in her palm. The crumpled currency notes, which had replaced the scars on the palms of her hands, radiated a gratifying sense of fulfilment. The vacuum in which she had once existed, where nothing new ever stirred, was being re-populated. Feelings and desires, culled from the fragments of her dreams, acquired outlines. She was like a boat, which had floated out of a pool of stagnant, stinking muck into a free-flowing crystalline river.

◆◆◆

Tapasi bought the books and started filling up the necessary forms to continue her education. Her lessons and her preparation for the exams once again became the major preoccupation of her life. Her suppressed but continuous thirst for higher study came to the fore again. The tender and reassuring words of Jaimala Devi, *'Mein hoon na'* were all the support she required. At times she felt as if Teacher Didi had risen from the ancient cemetery in Bolepur and come to her rescue. Wasn't that the reason why Jaimala Devi had taken charge of her life?

In retrospective moments Tapasi would find her soul tormented by memories of the unendurable pain that had almost annihilated her. Still, she was fully conscious of her role as a teacher to the children in the school and, as she taught, indulged and reprimanded them by turn, she was aware that she was giving them something. These children, like the starving children of Somalia, were being given a new lease of life, a new direction, education, knowledge—everything that her own childhood had been denied.

Tapasi was a very busy person. She worked hard. She prepared a variety of illustrated charts, made pictures and put them up on the walls. She drilled the concepts of discipline and cleanliness into the children and Jaimala Devi arranged for a doctor to give all the children and teachers regular medical examinations, hoping to improve their health. She wanted them in good health as much as Tapasi wanted them to have an education, which would make them aware individuals. Watching her, Jaimala Devi thought Tapasi was like a stream, not only cleansing her inner self, but also refreshing and energizing the whole school in the process.

Tapasi had known the dictionary meaning of words like 'happiness', 'radiance', and 'enthusiasm' but now she was beginning to experience them personally. Over time, and especially now that she had access to books, she felt herself gradually distancing herself from her past, from the insults and injuries that her psyche had suffered. The easy enthusiasm that she used to feel by the Chhatim Tila, gradually flowed back into her being. Studying books or teaching at school, Tapasi often thought about the fact that words and their meanings had been in existence for a very long time but she was only just beginning to understand them. And here she was, trying to convey words and their meanings from the books to the young children in school. How much could those poor, hungry children of downtrodden, illiterate parents, actually understand of what she was teaching?

Tapasi and Nandita often sat down with the children's parents and talked to them about life and its significance. But they were only snake charmers and charlatans. Was it fair to expect them to comprehend their words, when their only concern was with survival—with somehow filling their bellies and covering their nakedness? It was not realistic to expect them to have the desire, the discernment or the skills to look beyond these concerns. Still Tapasi told them, 'You should love your children. Pamper them. Show them that you care. Loving them is as important as feeding them. Your tender touch, your endearments are invaluable to the children.' She said all these things but was not sure if her words made any sense to them.

She wondered what more to do in order to prevent the children from living a life deprived of affection.

'Patience,' Jaimala Devi would advise her, 'Patience, Tapasi,' and Tapasi would wonder what patience was.

JAIMALA DEVI HAD rooted herself in the sacred soil of Vrindavan. Religion and social work were the *raison d'etre* of her life. But was she just living here or had she, in fact, completely given herself to *gopibhava*, the sentiment of the herdswomen, for Krishna? Tapasi sometimes felt that Jaimala Devi had succumbed to the mystique of the Kusum Sarovar. She would often tell Tapasi and the other women, 'The Lover and Beloved, (Krishna and Radha) often disport here under the Ashoklata bushes. Do you want to go, hide behind the undergrowth of the trees and watch them? Will you come with me?'

Indeed, Nandita and Uddhav had carried home her frail, half-conscious form from the steps of the pond on several occasions. Sometime she would say, 'A number of accomplished and noble sages reside in the groves around here. I have seen them sitting in meditation.' She would then herself sit in a posture of meditation, her eyes wide open but not seeing anything. She was a soft-spoken person who conversed gently with everyone and had won the hearts of all she knew. One day, she sent for Tapasi and when Tapasi arrived she said, 'Listen Tapasi, go and gather some Juhi flowers from those creepers over there and put them in a basket after counting them. I need a lakh of them for my

Agnihotri puja today.' Then she changed the topic abruptly. 'Kusum Sarovar is the playground of Krishna's female friends. They come here to frolic in the water and to gather flowers. Hurry, pluck the flowers before they arrive.' Tapasi glanced around her but, let alone Juhi creepers, there wasn't a single flowering plant in the vicinity. As she got up to go, Jaimala Devi said, 'Do you know, Tapasi, that Naradji bathed in this pond on one occasion? And, as a consequence, he was reborn as a woman! Don't you go bathing in that water,' she giggled.

Tapasi looked at her curiously. Later she went to Nandita and asked, 'What should I do, Nandita? From where will I obtain flowers for Jaimalaji's puja? Let alone flowers, the trees don't even have proper foliage here.'

'Don't worry, Tapasi. Uddhavji will get the flowers from the market. She conducts pujas like these every month. One day it is Tulsi puja, another day it is Ekadash or Poornima. All you do is count the flowers, which is a tough enough job in itself. To her Goverdhan is not a desolate ruin but a royal palace with a garden full of flowers. I don't know which world she dwells in and what its ambience is.'

'What do you know about Jaimalaji?' Tapasi was back to her dynamic, inquisitive self, her curiosity piqued by Jaimalaji's whimsical behaviour.

'I only know that she was born in Ujjain to a rich feudal family. She often talks about the sacred river Shipra and the Mahakaleshwar temple. Once she told me that her father was a subedar. Her education and training was entrusted to well-known scholars and tutors. She said her family followed strict discipline. She got up at four to go riding and spent the rest of the day in well regulated studies of art, philosophy and other subjects. And yes, she also told me that the original name of Ujjain was Avantika, and she grew up on the sacred soil where Krishna and his brother Balaram were educated.'

'And did she tell you that near Ujjain is the city of Vidisha where Agnimitra, the hero of Kalidasa's play *Malvikagnimitra*, who was also the second king of the Mauryan Empire, resided in the second century BC?' asked Tapasi.

'Yes, she did. There is a description of river Padmavati and the city of Kantipur near Gwalior in Bhavbhuti's famous play *Malathi Madhav*. Jaimalaji grew up and was educated in such wonderful places. She is not only a living history of life but also an embodiment of our ancient culture,' Nandita answered.

'I have heard that she is expecting a friend,' Tapasi changed the topic.

'Yes, she is arriving tomorrow. Ghanshyam has gone to Delhi to fetch her.'

Tapasi rushed off to find Uddhavji to ask him to arrange for the flowers. She was eager to see how so many flowers could be used in a puja. So far, the pujas, the bhajans, the cymbals and the interminable chanting of mantras had failed to bring about any spiritual transformation in her, but she was finding it difficult to dismiss Jaimala Devi's pujas and their rationale as mere absurdities. The expressive rituals, the fire offerings, and Jaimalaji's faith were knocking ever so insistently on Tapasi's consciousness.

◆◆◆

Jaimala Devi donned a gorgeous sari on the day the Tulsi puja was performed, and sat looking splendid in the traditional finery of a married woman. Everyone had pulled out their best saris. A tulsi plant, dressed in a gold-bordered red lehenga and dupatta, with a *shaligram* rock, a conch shell and other objects placed near it, was bathed in milk before being anointed with incense. Right through the ceremony, Jaimala Devi sang the *mangalachar*, the song of felicitation at a wedding, in her soft melodious voice. It was followed by the reading of *Katha*, a narration of a special story relating to the occasion. Tapasi listened attentively as Uddhavji read on, amidst a shower of *akshat* and flowers.

'In the battlefield after listening to the voice from the heavens, Deveshwar Shambhu confabulated with Sri Hari, who with his magical power assumed the garb of a Brahmin and obtained the most excellent armour from Shankhachoor. Thereafter, he moved toward Tulsi's palace in the form of Shankhachoor. Once he reached there his arrival was announced by the beating of the drums to the beauteous Tulsi. She watched from a window as he made his way on the main thoroughfare leading to the palace. She promptly distributed gifts and money amongst the Brahmins and asked them to recite verses of auspicious felicitations. She then began to adorn herself to welcome him. Bhagwan Vishnu, the solver of the problems of Gods and Goddesses, alighted from the chariot and entered the abode of Devi Tulsi. Tulsi worshipped God who had come in the guise of her husband, conversed with him and thereafter cohabited with him.

'However, that pious woman noticed some transgression in the enjoyment of pleasure and after dwelling on it for a moment, she grew suspicious. She began to shout, "Who are you? You wicked one, tell me who you are. You, who have consorted with me through deception, tell me who you are. You have violated and destroyed my chastity. I'll put a curse on you." The divine Lord transformed himself into his most enchanting form. Tulsi instantly recognized Vishnu incarnate but her marital chastity had been destroyed. So she told Bhagwan angrily, "Vishnu, you have a heart of stone with not an iota of pity in it. The violation of my vows of chastity by you implies that my husband is dead. Since you are cruel, merciless and wicked, so may you turn into a stone!" After pronouncing the curse, Shankhachoor's truly pious and devoted wife Tulsi broke down. Instantly, Bhagwan Shankar, who is the protector of His devotees, appeared and spoke to her. "Devi, listen to me now. All this is a consequence of the cause for which you did penance.

Lady, all that has happened was for that alone. You should cast your physical body away now and pass into a divine form. By the power of my blessings, Tulsi will be the major ingredient in the materials with which rituals of worship are performed. Lovely Lady, on earth, in the underworld and in heaven, you'll ever reside near Sri Hari. In heaven, you'll be the divine Goddess of trees who would ever disport with Sri Hari. As a consequence of your curse, Sri Hari, too would reside with you in the shape of a stone on the banks of river Gandaki in India. Any wise person who assembles a *shaligram* rock, Tulsi and a conch shell and takes care of them is beloved of Sri Hari."'

Jaimala Devi praised the Lord in a loud, clear voice and then offered *akshat*, flowers, sindoor and bangles to the Tulsi plant and showered her blessings on it for everlasting conjugal bliss. Tapasi sat and watched spellbound. Love, lovers, femininity, dalliances, conjugal bliss—these were all unfamiliar words. She thought of Jatin Da who was a storehouse of knowledge. He would have answered all her questions relating to these words but he was out of her life now so she hesitantly put the question to Nandita. 'Nanditaji, what is this thing called love? Is love the finest feeling in life?'

'I'll tell you what love is. Love is a longing that rises between a man and a woman. This desire is called energy in English and *oorja* in Hindi. It is the energy that sweeps gently over flowers, trees, our breath and the air around us, through rain and rivers, hills and valleys, and soaks them in serenity. But, in its rebellious moods it can destroy as well. People lose their senses when they are in love. They give everything to the object of their love.'

'When does love happen, Nanditaji?'

'When we meet the man of our dreams—the man we desire.'

'But all I have seen is husbands and wives fighting with each other. I have not seen them being loving. Does love really exist in this world?'

'Of course it does, Tapasi. Love is an intrinsic part of all our actions. Love is a powerful driving force in our lives. We break all bonds when we are in love. That is what I feel when I am in the arms of my Ranbir. In those moments, neither he nor I are what we are.' Nandita's whole being was suffused with the colour, and iridescent eloquence of passion.

'Maybe you are right. But I have no idea what love is,' Tapasi laughed abashedly and added, 'I have not been destined for love.'

'The body has certain needs, Tapasi. Sex is as essential to life as food to our belly.'

'Have you had sex or are you talking about it on the basis of what you have read in books?'

'Of course I have had sex, Tapasi. After marriage to

Ranbir, in the warmth of togetherness, I have experienced endless love. Maybe that is the reason why I always feel deep contentment in my heart.'

'Perhaps you do. But on the other hand, there's Uddhavji who is abusive and violent to his wife all the time. Each time I pass by his house, I find his wife going about her household work with a tear-stained face, muttering expletives under her breath and looking so agitated. But look at Uddhavji when he comes to school. He looks so dignified in his fine clothes with that tilak on his forehead, doesn't he?'

'Well, there are mismatched couples in the world too. But their existence does not change the definition of love. Love is an ever fresh, ever living feeling...' Nandita paused mid-sentence and then asked, 'But you were married, Tapasi. How come you...' She trailed off.

'Some people are born to be alone, Nanditaji. As was I. I know nothing about my mother or father. The only person I had to call my own was Kaka. But then he ganged up with Jatin Da and Kanika Di and sold me off as if I was nothing more than a shadow. A non-entity—a piece of rock, that's all. And then destiny tied my lot with one who was not even a man. He vented the resentment and frustration of his physical inadequacy on my body. Torturing me became his solace.'

Tapasi finally recounted the story of her past. After the whole story was out she felt drained and exhausted.

'Oh, Tapasi... You've put up with so much! How come you did not protest? You endured everything without complaint!'

'What does a seventeen or eighteen-year-old girl know about protest? Moreover, he drugged me. I don't know what he gave me but it was a pink powder mixed with milk. Once I discovered what he was up to the helplessness with which I had earlier endured all the humiliation converted into my strength. I felt as if I was being inspired by Ma Chamunda of Bamkhepa. When I stood up to him, he began to grow weaker. His complexes and frustrations then manifested themselves in the form of various illnesses and he died shortly thereafter. It is ironic that I, who had no suhag, still had to don a widow's weeds. The relatives in my marital family were only interested in his money, over which I had neither right nor control.'

Nandita held Tapasi's hand tightly. She said, 'Oh, Tapasi! Don't look back on the past now.' But Tapasi was lost in the past. At length she said softly, 'That is the perennial truth, Nanditaji, and what you have told me about love is the eternal untruth as far as my life is concerned. I have learnt that only selfishness is important in this world. Human beings are not. Their feelings do not matter and marriage is nothing more than a regulation under which women are placed.'

'Oh, you poor girl!' Nandita said and took her in her

arms. For the first time in all those years, the dam burst and Tapasi cried long and bitterly. All the pent-up grief and hurt gushed out.

Nandita stroked her back gently. 'Cry Tapasi. Let your tears wash away the bitterness inside you. Once you are cleansed of that, your inner resources will give you the energy to rise above the ordinary and help you become special. Your energy is yours and it has been prevented from falling prey to the politics of the body. By sublimating it you'll acquire a lot of strength.'

'Do you write poetry, Nanditaji?' Tapasi asked suddenly.

'Yes, I do. Poetry flows spontaneously when I am in a state of ecstasy.'

'Ecstasy? Is being ecstatic an incident that takes placc inside us? Or is it a delusion, or an expansion of our desires—an expansion without boundaries?'

'No, Tapasi. Ecstasy is a moment in time which becomes eternalized inside us. It is a moment of bliss, of joy. It is a moment of oblivion in which we are aware of nothing except our bodies. In that moment the world of reality dissolves into nothingness.'

Tapasi searched within herself to see if she had any such moments in her life. A day of pure joy—maybe the moments she had spent sitting under the shady trees of Vishwa Bharti. Or listening quietly to the conversations of students gathered at Didi's tea-stall. Yes, time did come to a standstill at such moments. Also something had melted inside her for a moment, fluttering like the wings of a butterfly, when she had first seen Malay after he returned from abroad. She had no recollection of the few childhood days she might have spent playing with him, but the thrill when they had collided that day had run through her body like an electric current. That was an unprecedented moment interwoven with pleasure. But before she could find an appropriate word to describe her burgeoning desire, Malay's white-skinned wife had trampled the tender petals of that moment with her high-heeled sandals and Tapasi had pushed her unnamed feeling into the deep abyss of death. However, to her consternation, today she realized suddenly that that subtle desire was still flickering in a corner of her heart. It had never been completely extinguished. It had not died out in spite of so much having transpired in her life.

Treading the memories of her past, Tapasi stopped and said, 'Shall I tell you something, Nanditaji? A lot of people used to gather at Jatin Da's house in the evenings. They were an assembly of so-called intellectuals. All kinds of subjects were discussed—from Rabindra Sangeet to Baul songs. For me, it was all a medium, an introduction to the ground realities of the world. On one occasion, an Urdu poet was also present in the gathering. Hardly anybody could understand his poetry so he decided to recite some lighter verse, one of which went:

"Merey janaze ke peechhe sara jahan nikla
Sirf woh na nikla jiske peechhe mera janaza nikla"

It is a convention that the audience repeats the verses of Urdu poetry after the poet. So one of the Bengali Babus repeated the lines like this:

"Merey janaze ke peechhe sara jahan nikla
Keval woh shala nahin nikla jiske peechhe mera Jenana nikla".'

Nandita and Tapasi burst out laughing.

WITTINGLY OR UNWITTINGLY, Tapasi was soon involved in Jaimala Devi's day-to-day life. She took on all of her big and small household chores. After school, she would wash and iron Jaimala Devi's clothes and clean her rooms. She stitched her Thakurji's clothes and trimmed them with golden lace and thoroughly enjoyed doing it. Her conversations with Jaimala Devi during this time revealed something of the mystery behind her life. Jaimala Devi learned Sanskrit from Nandita in the evenings. When Tapasi asked her why she was learning Sanskrit, she answered, 'One is never too old to learn something new. I want to read and understand Sanskrit classics myself. That is why I am studying it.'

Jaimala Devi had an inner awareness, which her face reflected and she was always eager for new experiences.

On one occasion, at a function in the school, the topic of discussion was music and art. Jaimala Devi revealed that she had learnt singing under the guidance of Rajpandit Shankar Govardhan Vidyadhar, the doyen of the Gwalior gharana. Besides, she had also trained in Kathak under the renowned Surendra Prasadji of Gwalior and learnt other dance forms from Navkumarji. Floating on the current of the memories of her past, she said, 'For me music was a way to transcend the world. It still is perhaps, because nothing can be more beautiful than music to relieve loneliness.'

Tapasi had adapted herself to Jaimala Devi's austere yet dynamic lifestyle. She found everything about her utterly attractive. She went to Jaimala Devi's room whenever she had time to spare. She wondered how a film star, accustomed to a glamorous lifestyle, could survive in such a modest house. Her room was hot as a furnace in summer but extremely cold in winter. Of course, she spent a few months of summer away in Delhi or Gwalior but she had made Goverdhan her home. During her absence, the school, the temple, Uddhavji and the others—all looked forlorn. Tapasi cleaned her room in her absence too. Sweeping the floor, removing cobwebs and dusting old books, she felt as if Jaimala Devi's frail old form was present in the room, offering her a hand in friendship. At such moments, Tapasi would sit very still and try to absorb Jaimala Devi's consciousness into the beating of her own heart. A lot of questions then turned into answers. The silence would grow eloquent and she could meditate on an idea, any idea, that had been knocking at her sensibility for long.

Once, when Tapasi was sorting out a trunk full of Jaimala Devi's old saris in her presence, her hand scraped a broken mirror wrapped in a silk scarf. She asked, 'Didi, shall I throw away this broken mirror?'

'Oh no, Tapasi. This mirror is a very important part of my past. It was fixed in the vanity case in which I carried my make-up. When shooting on location I put my make-up on with the help of this mirror. I had an accident on my last drive from Mumbai to Pune. To date no one knows whether it was an accident or someone had "organized" it. Anyway, I survived but the mirror broke. I felt that the breaking of the mirror was a sign, a decisive indication for a change of direction. So I salvaged this piece from the shards to add to my memorabilia. Let it be, Tapasi. This trunk holds a lot of memories. The pistol I got from the armoury of the royal family is also kept in it. Do you know something? In 1942, the revolutionaries used to come to people's homes for shelter at night. My father used to provide shelter to them. I was very young at that time and had no idea what their goals were but I was charmed by them. I had studied in an English school so I used to call them "jovial ghosts". That whole epoch was full of mystery, almost like a fairytale, to me. It was really thrilling to be part of it. To tell you the truth, those sort of committed revolutionaries, public personalities...leaders with their hearts bursting with patriotism...are not to be found today. Present day politics is screened off by a worn curtain, which you can see through with the naked eye.'

◆◆◆

Jaimala Devi's friend was coming to Vrindavan. Ghanshyam had escorted her down from Delhi in a taxi. She got off the taxi and came up to the veranda where Jaimala Devi was waiting to welcome her. The two ladies stood face to face in the small veranda. Tapasi noticed that they were the same age but very different from each other. The visitor was healthier and, though she was not beautiful, was quite fashionable. She had short hair, was tastefully made up and looked impressive in an expensive sari. In contrast, Jaimala Devi looked frail, spoke in a tremulous voice and wore an ordinary cotton sari. But her face was so beautiful. And those blue eyes—inviting people to drown themselves in limpid pools of compassion.

'Tapasi, could you arrange for tea, *beti*? Meet my childhood friend. We studied together at Miss Hill's school in Gwalior. The school was run by an American lady in those days.'

'Remember, Jaya, how you ran away from your rustic, old-fashioned, Sardar Putri Pathshala to get admission to our English school!'

They smiled and held hands. They seemed to have moved back to a special place in their past.

'I do too,' replied Jaimala Devi. 'And Grace, even at that tender age, I realized that the school was casting me in the mould of an ideal housewife—something that was totally unacceptable to me.'

'But I do remember that you got married after all,' said Grace.

'Yes I did, but I never accepted it. I remember how my Mamaji accompanied me with a loaded rifle when I was put on the train after my *gauna*. We had to travel down to Konkan. 1 was a graduate from St Xaviers and was keen to study further. I was not about to accept a life in Konkan as my destiny. I felt that a great injustice was being done to me. 1 could not live as a bride behind a veil. My decisive moment came when the train stopped at Kalyan station. I got off on the pretext of going to drink water, ran, and hopped onto a train that was pulling out of another platform. As luck would have it, it was a Pune bound train and my aunt lived there. 1 went straight to her house. She disapproved of my running away but since I had inflicted myself on her, she grudgingly decided to support me. She helped me find a job in Agarkar High School. My Bachelor's degree came in handy. I started teaching and became financially independent. I resumed my studies while I worked and in time went to Mumbai to take my Master's.'

'And it was during your trips to Mumbai that you met Mr Karve who used to write screenplays and dialogues for the movies....'

'Yes, he encouraged me to join films and helped me get the role of the heroine in Baburam Prabhakar's first film, *La Pandava*. Maybe that was my destiny, Grace. Frail leaves are carried away by storms—they can't remain fixed to trees. I too was carried away by the glittering world of glamour.'

'You were exceedingly beautiful, Jaya. Sorry, you still are. The ruins are a testimony to the grandeur of the beautiful edifice!'

They started laughing and suddenly, for the first time, Tapasi realized what civilized and genteel laughter meant. The sound of their laughter was sweet and low, like the tinkling of silver bells.

Nandita, who happened to be sitting cross-legged on a dhurrie on the floor, chipped in, 'Which other films did you act in? Do tell us, Jaimalaji.'

'A whole lot of films,' Grace answered for Jaimala Devi. 'There was *Sikandar* with Prithviraj Kapoor which brought you a lot of fame, Jaya. People went crazy over the Rukhsana of that film. I was abroad at that time but I read about you in the magazines.'

Grace paused at a page in the book of the past and Jaimala Devi took over from her. 'And after that movie, my leading men would address me variously as "Diana" and "Moon Goddess"! Once, when I was riding a horse during the shooting of a movie, Prithvirajji watched me coming down the slope of a hill. Admiring my riding skills, he commented, "Her parents must have put her on a saddle instead of in a cradle!" As a matter of fact, riding, which I had learned in my girlhood, came in handy during my career. Moreover, I could adapt myself to any role with spontaneity. They never needed a double for me.'

It was time to feed the birds. Jaimala Devi walked out onto the veranda with a basket in her hands and Grace followed her. Hordes of birds began to descend around them, fluttering down from different directions. Tapasi loved the spectacle. Every bird had the right to live. Grace, Tapasi and Nandita watched entranced as Jaimala Devi scattered the grain to feed the birds. The colourful birds seemed to lift their parted beaks as if blowing kisses to the lovely lady who fed them.

The woman helper brought tea in two discoloured glasses and snacks in an old stainless steel plate. Even the table on which they were served was quite rickety.

'Come, Grace. Have some tea,' Jaimala Devi said, reoccupying the chair from which she had risen.

'Jaya, all the female artistes from your time are still working as character actors in the roles of mother, aunt or grandmother. But you quit after...what was that film for which you got the President's Award? And then you gave up everything, to come and live here, in the back of beyond, like an ascetic!'

'Yes, Grace,' answered Jaimalaji in her sweet, gentle voice. 'After doing a significant role like that of Shyamchi Ayee, I felt that I would not be able to accept the run-of-the mill roles any longer. After having tasted the sublime I could not bring myself to depict those lowly, functional characters. The decision to quit was a split-second one. I quit and, wrapped in the warmth of the moment, came here.' She was silent for a while, then continued, 'It was extremely difficult to establish myself here at first. There were so many problems. And yet, I'm bound to the cruel reality of this place—to the chirping of these birds, to these lively pathways of Vrindavan, to these winding lanes of Mathura, Goverdhan Parvat and to the anguish of girls like Tapasi.' She looked affectionately at Tapasi.

'Haven't you ever felt any regret, Jaya? Some remorse?'

'As an answer to your question Grace, I'll recite an Urdu couplet which actor KN Singh often used to quote:

"Shikvey nahin kissi sey magar haan malaal hai
Kuchh agli pichhli baaton ka behbak khyaal hai."

Packing in its radiance, the sun was about to close shop and set in the mysterious depths of the sky. The day was tiredly blending into dusk. Grace took her leave from Jaimala Devi and Kusum Sarovar. Tapasi went up to the taxi to see her off. While the westernized guest drove away to her material world, Jaimala Devi busied herself lighting the oil lamps for the *aarti* in the darkness of her room. Soon the words of the aarti floated out, scattering into the air like birds fluttering over the calm serenity of Kusum Sarovar.

THERE WAS A commotion outside. Ghanshyam, the temple priest was saying something anxiously. Nandita and Tapasi came running out of their respective classrooms and Gayatri stopped the new song she was teaching the children midway. The notes from the abruptly closed harmonium hung in the air. The entire school hurried towards Uddhavji's temple. A crowd had already gathered in the courtyard where Ghanshyam and the others were talking nonstop. The focus of excitement was Mauni Baba's frail body lying on the ground in a swoon.

Ghanshyam said, 'Baba came outdoors regularly. He took a walk or headed towards the market. But he had not come out for the last two or thee days.'

The priest added, 'He goes to Kusum Sarovar for a bath at dawn. At times, he sits and meditates on the steps of the pond. A disciple of his also comes from somewhere at the same time. After Baba goes inside his room, the disciple stands outside the door and pronounces *Jai Radhey* twice and prostrates himself to pay obeisance. Mauni Baba does not speak, but the echoes of the disciple's own voice seem to return from under the floor of Baba's room. This morning the disciple got worried when he got no reply to his *Jai Radhey* so he informed me. I thought that Baba had taken a vow of silence but I have often been witness to him being in a state of trance and lying for hours in a state of oblivion.'

A query rose instantly to Tapasi's mind. 'What is a state of oblivion?'

By now the senior Uddhavji had arrived. 'Please don't crowd around Baba. Mauni Baba is not unconscious. He is in a state of divine ecstasy.'

Ecstasy? Tapasi grew curious about Baba.

The crowd was dispersed. Gayatri led the children back to their classrooms. Baba's disciple arrived accompanied by a vaid who was dressed in a dhoti-kurta. He checked Baba's pulse and instructed the people to lift him from the ground and lay him down on the sun-drenched platform.

'Since when has he been unconscious?' he asked.

The disciple answered, 'It has been coming for a few days. I had last visited two or three days ago. His door was open and I saw him inside, in a state of frenzy. He laughed and cried by turns. I left a vessel full of milk for him and went back.'

'Did Baba drink the milk?' someone asked.

'Yes he did. The vessel was empty this morning but Baba was found lying here like this. So I went and fetched vaidji.'

'You won't understand how spiritually elevated Baba is. He remains constant in his devotion and gets into ecstatic, trancelike states frequently. I have often seen the glow of a large oil lamp at midnight in his room. And if you were to go check it out, you wouldn't find any lamp there. So how do you explain the light?' Uddhav asked.

The vaid tried to to mix some powder with a bit of water and pour it into Baba's mouth but the water seeped out.

'Has he taken any food and drink?' asked the vaid rubbing a yellowish paste on Baba's palms.

'He hardly eats anything. A few days ago when he was in a similar state, I had taken him to a doctor in Radha Kund. I'd brought prasad for him from a temple in Gwalior but he'd refused it and wrote to me on his slate, " I shall not eat anything from the raja." He only drinks milk.'

'At times, he even takes arsenic with milk,' someone revealed. The vaid was astonished. 'In that case he is not likely to survive. The slow poison is going to take its toll. Anyway, I'm leaving these powders. Give them to him mixed with water and apply these pastes on his palms and the soles of his feet. It'll prevent the arsenic from spreading further. The rest is God's will. I'll come back in the evening to check him out.'

The vaid picked up his bag and left and the people began to move away from the scene. The priest and Mauni Baba's disciple continued to tend to him but he opened neither his mouth nor his eyes. Only his slow breathing continued, making his body tremble gently.

'Uddhavji, you must know how long Mauni Baba has been living here?' Tapasi's question could not hold itself back.

'Yes, of course I know that he has been living here for quite a few years. But he is not a native of Brijbhumi. He had originally come from Orissa to study here. He comes from a family of Oriya sages of the *Madhya gauriya* sect. I don't know his real name but I remember that he was well known for his garrulousness in the gurukul where he studied. He didn't sit quiet even while studying. On one occasion when he was talking nonsense, his teacher reprimanded him saying, "Keep quiet, stupid!" Since that moment silence has been his language. Earlier he used to live in a forest two miles away but for some years he has been living here. We, the people in this area, built this shelter for him. All he does is live in his deep silence and drink milk laced with arsenic. He has no friends and no enemies.'

After finishing their work at school, Tapasi and Nandita went back to see how Mauni Baba was doing. He was still unconscious. Uddhavji and Ghanshyam had called a doctor to examine him. The doctor gave him an injection but there was no change in Baba's condition. All those who saw him wondered where and in whom his consciousness was centered. People sitting by him seemed to be waiting for the moment when Baba would pass into eternal silence. Gangajal, tulsi and an unbaked clay diya were kept ready by his side. The priest had opened the doors of the temple and was singing a bhajan in subdued tones. Time moved slowly. After a while, Nandita left for home and Tapasi sat alone on the steps watching the scene. Suddenly, a young boy, about ten or twelve years of age and dressed in a white dhoti and short kurta, came bouncing into the courtyard of the temple. He waved his hands about and enquired, 'Where is the Oriya Baba who is about to die?'

Uddhavji said, 'This is the Goswamiji of Barsana's son. What brings him here, and unaccompanied at that?'

The boy held up a small packet in his hand and said, 'Feed this paan to Baba. It has been sent by Shriji. He told me in a dream last night, "Oriya Baba of Kusum Sarovar has not been able to bear the radiance of my darshan. He is on his deathbed. Go and feed him a *prasadi beeda* from me. He'll come back to life."'

Before anybody could react and laugh at the child's innocent prattle or make any comment, he sprinted away from the crowd of spectators, approached the place where Baba was lying and unpacked the paan from its leaf wrapping. He touched Baba's mouth with it. And lo and behold! Baba's lips moved and the colour began to return to his face! Echoes of his disciples' voices pronouncing '*Jai Radhey*' began to break the silence of Baba's unoccupied room. People ran towards the room. The child left exactly the way he had come and was soon out of sight. Mauni Baba opened his eyes and turned over on his side. The pujari offered him some water to which the medicinal powder had been added and Baba drank it in quick gulps. Many voices were heard exclaiming simultaneously, 'The injection has taken effect at last.'

'Perhaps Baba has come out of his trance.'

Uddhavji's voice rose above them all, 'Where has that child gone? Go, look for him,' and he could be seen trembling and rushing off to find the boy. 'Oh, where is that child?'

'Bankey Bihari, Jai Krishna Kanhai'. The disciple helped Baba to rise. Baba looked as if he had woken from deep sleep. He surveyed the crowd with surprise and walked into his room.

A woman's voice declared, 'Kanha had come to meet Baba who had been missing him.'

Very soon the silence emanating from Baba's room began to pervade the atmosphere outside. The number of visitors to the Uddhav Mandir grew steadily. Offerings, cow's milk for Baba, disciples bringing *charnamrit* from the seven houses of God ...all these added to Baba's fame. The folklore surrounding him grew and assumed more and more fantastic forms as it spread far and wide. Believing devotees and sceptical devotees in need of solace began to converge upon the temple from all over.

Baba resumed answering questions. Everybody valued the relevance and gravity of his answers. Because he bathed in the Kusum Sarovar, the faithful began to drink its water believing it to be *charnamrit*.

The compound of the school became a camping ground for pilgrims flocking to see Baba. Jaimala Devi had been away in Delhi when the miracle occurred. On her return, she was grieved to learn that she had missed the darshan of the manifestation of child Krishna. As for Tapasi, though she had been witness to the whole incident, she was still sceptical about it. Pondering the various instances of death she had seen, she wondered what it was like to transit through the ephimerality of one's own existence.

JAIMALA DEVI HAD, with great difficulty and much persuasion, been coaxed to open the floodgates of memory. Nandita had merely asked her once or twice, but Tapasi's inquiring, analytical self couldn't refrain from asking questions.

For a long moment, Jaimala Devi seemed to stand swamped by the memories stored in her mind. At length she began to speak:

'You have dug open my past which had been buried for years. One may wander around for miles in the wilderness of memories and still get nothing substantial. All you obtain are some painful, dusty memories moist with tears that never stop.'

She was silent for a moment, then continued: 'I left the natural serenity and academic life of Pune and came to live in the fast-paced and exciting world of Mumbai. To stumble was inevitable and so I moved into it with open arms prepared to drown.

'A film actress has a very lonely existence, Tapasi. Her passion finds an outlet only on screen. Her real life is full of silence, sadness and loneliness, because she is cut off from mainstream life. Even if she wants to remain connected to real life, she can't. All the publicity and praise printed in the magazines, honours, and rewards...are superficial things. Actresses have to stifle their inner selves and kill their desires. Ironically, it is only through their bodies that the beauty and talent inherent in them can be expressed. So all their time and energy is spent maintaining and enhancing their appearance at the cost of their natural desires. Isn't it strange that we possess a body, which we deny constantly?

'Once I got into the world of films, I began to feel that my figure and face had become a bankable commodity to my social circle and relatives. I was up for sale. This was so because one has to depend on several men in this profession. That dependence is unavoidable. We had to identify with everybody—producers and directors, heroes and villains. A film is the result of teamwork. It is like a family enterprise. But it is also a fact that these men had no qualms about exploiting heroines sexually because for them, whoever bedded the heroine of the film was the winner of the team. Not many people appreciated another's triumph.'

Jaimala Devi was trying to rationalize her past life.

'Flowing along with the current, I found myself attracted to Karve Saheb. Maybe I fell in love with him. With his backing I descended deeper into the abyss of the film world, without thinking of its implications. Karve Saheb was a serious kind of man...a genius. He was suave and charming and I cherished the affectionate way he treated me. He was highly educated. I found his habit of contemplation quite irresistible. I was aware of the dangers of falling in love with a married man because to him his family was of paramount importance. Then how about my love? He returned my love in the manner of a rich man tossing small change at a beggar.

My devotion had no value, none at all. To him, I was a convenience. Whenever he found some free time—a few moments, a few hours off—he would spend it with me as a reward for my boundless love for him. The nights used to be terribly lonely for me. My heart, my nerve centre—everything was like a haunted house—desolate and echoing with the sound of the wind. He took charge of my career, selected my roles, what to do and when, which movie to sign and which one to reject—he took all those decisions. He also managed my finances. He had full control over what I earned and how I spent it. My flat, my car and all my personal expenses were handled by him. My lack of worldliness became a powerful weapon in his hand and he used it against me. On one occasion, my role in a film landed me into legal trouble. Since I was naive, I lost the case. Karve Saheb, who was present when the verdict was pronounced, slapped me across the face in full view of the entire courtroom. For a moment I was stunned. After that the whole universe, its speed and its gravity as well as the rainbow hues of love seemed to crash around me like splintered glass.'

Tears rolled down from Jaimala Devi's blue eyes like shattered dreams. The memory of that humiliating moment seemed to choke her. Tapasi offered her a glass of water, which she drank quickly. Jaimala Devi's feet were still planted on the grainy terrain of her past. She composed herself and resumed after a few moments, 'Standing in the witness box, I was stung with anger and humiliation. Then taking all my courage in my hands, I planted a resounding slap on Karve Saheb's face. His spectacles flew off his nose and crashed on to the floor. Now it was his turn to be stunned. There was a shocked silence in the courtroom as I rushed out of there wordlessly.'

Jaimala Devi's anguish revealed itself in the beads of perspiration that suddenly dotted her face. She looked drained, but she continued, 'That, Tapasi, was the moment of reckoning for me. It was an eye-opener. That final touch of Karve Saheb's hand brought me back to reality. My eyes were opened. I did not merely see but also realized that I had nothing despite having acted in so many box office hits and winning so many awards. The flat where I stayed was not in my name nor was any other roof under which I could live. Enquiries at the bank revealed that no account had ever been opened in my name. So the star-queen of the screen stood like a pauper in the marketplace—empty-handed, defeated. I had some jewellery which I sold and then I just quit everything—new films, new producers who chased me till here, all those actors who were dying to work with me. I simply turned my back on my life of fantasy and glamour.

What followed was a very painful phase, Nandita. I remained in a state of mental breakdown for I don't know how long. On one occasion a money order for a hundred rupees came from Karve Saheb, which I promptly returned.' She closed her eyes for a moment. 'A frightful sense of humiliation ran through my veins like a fever. A throbbing pain tormented my sensibility. I was weak and vulnerable and I kept falling ill. I would curse the meaninglessness of my existence. Why did I have to fall in love? Why did I believe he too loved me? Such questions haunted me all the time. But one's mind stops thinking when one is in love. At any rate, what business did I have to love a married man? Anyhow, at that time I was obsessed with love. That is all. It took me time to understand, Tapasi, that most men and women are not mature enough emotionally to grasp the greatness of a feeling like love. It is more like play-acting than love for them. Most individual men and women love only themselves. They exploit each other for their own physical gratification. Love and marriage are just a farce of self-seeking pursuits. Believing in something other than this was a big mistake and a big insult to myself. Tapasi and Nandita, that insult still hounds me.'

Adrift in a sea of memories, Jaimala Devi seemed to experience some of them all over again and exhausted, lay down.

All this talk got Nandita thinking about her own experience of love. She was convinced that her husband Ranbir loved her for herself. His devotion to her was her deepest, most intimate joy. She nurtured her love in a spiritual sense too.

Presently, Jaimala Devi rose and sat in a chair sipping her tea. The whole place resounded with the song of the crickets. In the distance a few fireflies played hide and seek among the Oleander trees. Tapasi sat on the steps near Jaimala Devi's room and thought about what Jaimala Devi had said. 'What is love? A deception, a shadow, a fleeting fancy or something more.'

Just then Ghanshyam entered the house holding a sheaf of papers in his hand. He said, 'Didiji, your tickets for Delhi have arrived. You have to leave tomorrow evening. I have arranged for a taxi too.'

'Jaya Didi, what do you do in Delhi?' Tapasi asked pensively.

'My mission in Delhi is to promote the life, history and teachings of Chhatrapati Shivaji Maharaj on a national level. That is what I do in Delhi, Tapasi. We also publish a magazine from there.'

'But this place is so forlorn when you are away,' said Tapasi.

'I have two goals in life, Tapasi. One is spiritual and the other material. When I go to Delhi I work as much as I can—I write articles for magazines. Then centered in materialism, I get glimpses of the raslila of Kunj Bhihari through my mind's eye and I really enjoy it. Moreover, it is my mission to collect money for our school.'

'When will you return?'

'I'll be back soon. In time for Swami Haridas Jayanti's music concert.'

How frail she looks, thought Tapasi, sensing that, to a large extent, Jaimala Devi was withdrawing from material objects to focus on her inner being. She seemed to be melting away in her love of Sri Kunj Bihari Ji. She observed so many fasts. Once when Tapasi asked her why she fasted so often, she had answered, 'A fast is a psychological reminder of hunger. If we are mindful of suffering or of hunger, we acquire a kind of power. Nature also helps us in coping with self-denial. Add the name of God to that and we are energized and our view of suffering and hunger undergoes a change.' She stopped and asked abruptly, 'How old are you, Tapasi?'

'Why do you ask?' Tapasi countered but made some quick mental calculations. Married at sixteen, two years of marriage, then three years in the Widow's Home followed by four in the service of the school during which she had cleared her matric and taken the BA exam. '1 am twenty-five, Didi.'

'Oh my God! So young! And are you going to spend the rest of your life in the gloomy loneliness of your little room here?'

"What else can I do? When I look back, I realize that this is the first time I have had a chance to live for myself. I'm working in the school and studying. I was crazy about studying ever since I was a child. Living with the children, I feel I was destined to be here and that is how I've travelled to this far away place.' She did not wish to delve into her past, so she added, 'And what I cherish most here is your company which is something absolutely invaluable. The moment my BA results come out I want to appear for the GMAT exam. Jaya Didi, you have done so much for me. Please help me go abroad for higher studies too.'

'Yes, of course, I'll help as much as I can. My niece in Delhi is a lecturer in a college. She can definitely help you.'

Ghanshyam, who had been listening to their conversation spoke up at last, 'Tapasi, I've been waiting here with this newspaper for so long but you haven't even noticed me, I ran to tell you, the result is out...'

'Really?' Tapasi snatched the newspaper from his hand and spread it out on the floor. She scanned it for her roll number and immediately stood up with tears rolling down her cheeks. 'Jaya Didi...Jaya Didi...'

"What has happened? Why are you crying? Tell me!'

'Jaya Didi, I have passed with the highest marks in the university!'

'What wonderful news! And still you are crying! You are crazy, aren't you?' Jaimala Devi put an affectionate hand around Tapasi's shoulder and turning to a beaming Ghanshyam, said, 'Run to the market and get some sweets. Also arrange tickets for Tapasi, too. I'm taking her to Delhi with me!'

Tapasi said, 'Let me go and inform Mauni Baba,' and rushed off cheerfully.

◆◆◆

A large number of people were bathing at the Kusum Sarovar completely absorbed in their rituals. Their lives followed the usual self-seeking preoccupations.

As Tapasi stood there her attention was diverted by a large, colourful butterfly floating on the breeze. The butterfly fell in front of her. Tapasi stopped in her tracks. She picked up the butterfly and tried to make it fly again but the butterfly was dead. Its wings were still. She wished she could ask the butterfly where it had come from and where it had been bound. Where was its home? In what garden did it sleep on its petal bed? Under what green tree? What flower? But the questions remained unasked. She placed the fragile dead creature in a niche in a crumbling wall and covered it with sand to form a little grave that no feet would desecrate.

Mauni Baba's courtyard was crawling with people. There was no way she could reach him at that time so she retraced her steps. She halted in front of Uddhavji's temple. She wished to make a prayer for the butterfly or maybe for her own future. She murmured some words tentatively. She had never tried to memorize the jaaps and knew her words were meaningless. She returned to her room quietly. When she entered she saw a slip of paper lying on her table. It was from Mauni Baba. She opened it and read the following words: 'Efforts made with sincerity and confidence are never unfruitful.'

TAPASI WENT OFF with Jaimala Devi to Delhi to prepare for and to take the GMAT exam. She was looked after very well and given a separate room to prepare for the exam. Once, tired from studying, she looked pale and Jaimala Devi insisted on taking her for a blood test.

Tapasi returned to Vrindavan after a month. She looked content and calm, as if the GMAT was not an exam but an instrument through which her doubts had been dispelled and her questions answered. She resumed her work at school. The moment Nandita saw her she exclaimed, 'Tapasi! looks like Delhi has left its mark on you. How different you look! You look so good, so attractive!'

Tapasi was pleased but she said, 'You are teasing me.'

'Why should I? You really look great. More confident and polished than ever! So smart and beautiful!'

'I stayed with Jaya Didi's niece Vasundhara for a month. She said I looked too much of a country girl and if I were to live in Delhi I had to change my way of dressing. She got new clothes stitched for me. She also taught me how to drape a sari elegantly. She took me to a "parlour" and got me to trim my hair. With a hair cut and light make-up I looked so different I thought it was someone else! I was no longer the old "Taposhi" who was chided for laughing in an uncouth manner and dismissed from Malay's presence like a servant! I was no longer the girl ravaged by that hideous black woman in the Widow's Home.'

Nandita's eyes welled up with tears. 'You should put all that behind you, Tapasi. Are you going to work in Delhi now?'

'Yes, I will. Vasundharaji said I could stay with her. She is not married yet. She is not too well but I don't know what her health problem is. Anyway, it hardly matters where I stay once I begin to work. I've always dreamt about Vishwa Bharti. That dream remains unfulfilled. I will be in a position to take a final decision only after the GMAT results are declared. My result will determine my escape.'

'Escape or progress?'

'I don't know.'

◆◆◆

Tapasi was about to head off to her class when she suddenly remembered the dead butterfly she had buried before going to Delhi. She rushed outside, reached the crumbling wall where the grave of the butterfly was, and stirred the sand gently. The butterfly looked as beautiful as it had on the day it died. Its velvety body and the colours of its wings glowed clean, clear and brilliant. Does it mean that change does not affect the body in death? Does beauty remain frozen in the body? But what about the body of the Mahantji that had been installed in that underground cellar in a state of *samadhi*? And the overpowering stench that rose from it? How does one explain that?

Tapasi placed the butterfly on the palm of her hand. She had barely begun to caress its wings with her fingers when they fell apart like dry leaves. The velvety body crumbled into a tiny pile of ash. Tapasi decided that it was time to bid goodbye to her painful past and come to terms with the truth of the present moment. The ashes of the butterfly on the palm of her hand were a witness to that truth. She would immerse them in the water of Kusum Sarovar.

The butterfly was a unit of the gigantic magnificence of Nature. It flowed along with the current of the world, like she herself had, because to float upstream was not possible for it, for Tapasi, or for anyone else. But there are other directions stretching endlessly. It is possible for individuals to find different directions.

SHE WAS DESCENDING the steps of Kusum Sarovar when she heard someone call out, 'I say, it is our Taposhi! Hey, you're Taposhi, aren't you? What are you doing here?'

Tapasi looked up immediately, at once placing the distinctive Bolepur Bengali accent. The powdered remains of the butterfly slipped through her fingers and fell into the pond.

'Bholanath Kaka! How come you are here? How's everybody at home?' The memories of the past, which she had hoped to submerge in the water, began instead to surge like blood through her veins.

'Don't you remember our Chhote Babu? Malay? You used to play with him as a child.'

Vilayati Babu Malay, the husband of the white woman. What brought him to Vrindavan, the wilderness for widows? Her nerves grew taut.

'Chhote Babu, this is Taposhi... Rakhal's niece. Remember she used to come to the house to help Didi Ma with the housework? How Didi Ma loved her!' Bholanath was really excited to see her.

'How come you are here, Taposhi?' Malay asked.

'I am a widow.' Her voice grew stony. She turned quickly and ran up the steps of Kusum Sarovar. Bholanath and Malay followed her. She wanted to have nothing to do with them but they would not leave her alone. She turned to see them following her.

'When did you come here?' she asked finally.

'Only yesterday.'

Tapasi took them to the school and up to her room. 'Come in, Bholanath Kaka. You too Malay, if you wish. I live here.' Her body tingled as she spoke his name.

Malay's eyes lingered on her. It was as though he was seeing her for the first time. A slender, delicately carved figure. Long, thick, lustrous hair, enormous, eloquent eyes with a mysterious luminosity, a radiant brow, a face innocent of make-up but captivatingly attractive. So different from the coarse wild child of Bolepur. What a transformation—from a non-entity to a living woman, typically Indian and so beautiful.

'Come, Bhaiya, let us rest for a while. You have been on your feet since yesterday,' Bholanath said to Malay, then turning to Tapasi he said, 'It is great to see you after such a long time, Taposhi.'

Malay followed Bholanath into Tapasi's room. It was a very simple but neat and tidy room. There was a bed covered with a clean sheet, a chair and a table with a reading lamp and a large shelf full of books mounted on the wall. In a corner of the room stood a small stove and a small food cabinet covered with wire mesh which contained sundry pots and pans. Everything was simple and yet marked with a lot of character.

Malay sat on the bed while Bholanath took the chair. And Tapasi? She was too nervous to sit. The sudden replay of her distant past had thrown her off balance. She rushed down and instructed Ghanshyam to arrange for refreshments. Returning, she prepared tea on the stove and poured it into glasses. She said, 'I don't have much to offer, but whatever I do is here for you.'

'Oh, don't say that. It is such a nice room. My God, so

many books! You read so much, do you?'

Tapasi nodded. The old diffidence darkened her eyes.

'She was so good at her studies, Chhote Babu. She always topped her class. She was married off at a very young age otherwise...' Bholanath trailed off.

'If she was so intelligent, why the hurry to get her married? Child marriage? How come Dada didn't prevent it? Hasn't that obsolete system been banished yet?'

'She didn't want to get married. It was that Kaka of hers—the drunken sod, Rakhal, who took a lot of money from Majumdar. She was forced to marry him.'

'Rakhal Kaka was not the only one involved in bartering me, was he?' Tapasi asked quietly.

'What can I say? I am only a servant, Taposhi. And there is no point talking about it because both of them have left this world. May they rest in peace.'

'What are you saying?' Tapasi sank down and sat on the mat. 'Tell me Kaka, you mean Jatin Da and Kanika Di...?' She could not bring herself to complete the sentence.

'Yes, Taposhi, they have both gone. Jatin Da fell seriously ill soon after your wedding. He used to have terrible pain in his abdomen. Dr Ghosh treated him for eight to ten months. He was admitted to the big hospital. Ma left no stone unturned to get him well. Medical treatment, exorcism, tantrik rituals, prayers—everything was tried but Dada could not be saved. He suffered a great deal, Taposhi.'

Tapasi was crying. Her face was drenched in tears. She looked at Malay and said, 'You should have taken him abroad. They have so many medical facilities there...'

'I could not come, Taposhi. Ma had asked me to come but Lillian was in the hospital with our premature baby. It was impossible to leave them in that condition,' Malay said regretfully.

Bholanath resumed, 'Didi Ma was in a state of shock at Dada's passing away. She went into deep depression. She used to call out to you. She would talk to herself. Over time, her health failed and she wasted away and finally died. Chhote Babu could not come even then. I had to manage everything on my own. All the arrangements, funeral rites like puja and *shraadh*—I managed them to the best of my capacity.'

Tapasi could not stop the tears. Her face grew flushed as she asked Malay, 'Why didn't you come? How could you neglect your mother for the sake of your Memsahib and your child? That too, a mother who lived for you! I remember how everytime she cooked your favourite dishes or made your favourite snacks, she would think about you. How could you forget a mother so loving?' She fell silent but the tears continued to roll down her cheeks. After a while she spoke again, 'Forgive me, Malay Babu, I have no right to say these things. I am sorry. It is a fact that I loved and respected Kanika Di deeply. She was like a mother to me. That is why I can understand how restless she must have felt in her lonely house. How she must have missed you and longed to see her grandchild! How could you cast off your Indian *sanskaras*?' She broke down again, then recovering, she said, 'Please forgive me. I have no right to speak to you like this. I am nobody. Do forgive me. I said all these things because I know how heartbroken she must have been.'

'Taposhi, please go on talking. It is reassuring to me that there is someone in this world who can talk to me as if it is her right to ask for an explanation—someone who is reproaching me. I've been so lonely since I have returned. I've not be able to share my grief with anybody except Bholanath... all that has happened to me, in my life...'

'Have you come alone? How about your mem—sorry, your wife and child?'

Malay's face grew sad. He stared at the blank wall before him and answered, 'I've come alone. They are not a part of my life anymore. The baby did not survive. Afterwards, Lillian and I were divorced. A few months were needed to sort out all those problems. By the time I settled everything and came here, it was all over.'

'I am sorry,' Tapasi said. The three of them sat quietly, each with their own thoughts. She had never spoken at such length to Malay before. The old childhood days when they'd played together were long forgotten.

Ghanshyam brought food for the guests. A rickshaw-puller dressed in a coloured vest and shorts helped him carry up the food. Tapasi took out a clean sheet from her trunk and spread it on the straw mat. Food was served in green leaf plates. Puri, katchori, subzi, chutney and earthenware pots full of curd and rabri.

'You have got so much food for us, Taposhi! We could have eaten somewhere in the market.'

'In the market here? You wouldn't be able to eat in the market at all. It is so dirty. Don't you remember how many times Kanika Di made you wash your hands at mealtimes?' Tears welled up in Tapasi's eyes again. '1 don't have forks and spoons, you'll have to eat with your fingers.'

Malay was deeply moved by Tapasi's mixed feelings of joy and sorrow. He began to eat as if in a trance. He looked at Tapasi and said, 'You should eat, too.'

'Later,' she replied.

Ghanshyam had brought bottles of cold drinks, which he opened after the meal and offered to the guests. Bholanath turned to him and asked, 'Will you tell us where and how to go about *tarpan* and other such things?'

'Sure. My father arranges those rituals. Whose *tarpan* is due? A man or a woman?'

'Neither a man nor a woman. We have come here to perform the *tarpan* of the spirits of the dead.'

'What did you say?' Ghanshyam flopped onto the floor with a thud.

Tapasi's hands froze. A profound silence descended upon the room. The guests continued to eat in silence. Tapasi handed a clean towel to Malay. She removed the leftover food and put it away in a corner of the room. Returning, she resumed her position on the mat.

'What did you say, Kaka? Whose *tarpan* do you want to perform?'

I'll not keep it from you, Taposhi. I'll tell you all. Chhote Babu could not come home even after Didi Ma's death. I arranged for everything according to my means and my understanding. Not a single friend from among those who used to enjoy Dada's lavish hospitality turned up. After the funeral rituals, I locked up the house and put a big lock on the gate. As long as Didi Ma had lived I had got my meals and salary from that house. I had to take up another job after she passed away. I went back to the house every now and then to water the garden but I never opened the door of the house.

'Now, when Chhote Babu arrived after three years, I handed the house keys to him. The lock on the door had grown rusty. I'm telling you the truth, Taposhi. When we entered the house, we found it exactly as it was when I locked it up. It was absolutely neat and clean and everything looked bright and shiny Not a trace of dust, cobwebs or trash anywhere! And do you remember Dada's brass hookah? Its shine had not dimmed at all, it sent forth a familiar aroma of tobacco and the water in its container was still warm! Shall

I tell you more? There were fresh flowers on the idol of Ma in Didi Ma's temple. The Gangajal was full to the brim and there was a burning incense stick. As if Didi Ma had just left after peforming puja.'

'You are kidding, Kaka! How can that be? You have invented stories which can't be believed in the modern age.' Tapasi tried to laugh. There must have been somebody... maybe Shivdei who used to put oil in Didi's hair...or one of her friends...Chitra or someone else. Somebody must have been visiting the house unknown to you.'

'No, Taposhi. No one ever came. All the doors and windows were firmly locked. Chhote Babu opened everything with his own hands.'

Malay confirmed Bholanath's claim. 'It was amazing. I was so surprised. There was no door open to allow access to anyone. Anyway, I'm going to stay there for ten or fifteen days when I go back. But when I went to the house, I sensed a presence. I could hear footsteps. I don't know whose they were. Maybe Ma comes and sits at the head of my bed or lights incense sticks in the temple. I feel someone breathing close to me, near my head on the pillow. Taposhi, I can feel somebody breathing. Really, I can. It is true.' Malay seemed to be convincing not only Tapasi but also himself.

The silence grew deeper.

Ghanshyam spoke at last, 'Why don't you ask Mauni Baba what it means in the evening? He is well reputed for his wisdom. He'll enlighten you.'

'Yes, Taposhi, ask him. We have come here after hearing about him. We have heard that he has virtually returned from the door of death. His fame has spread far and wide.'

'I am surprised his reputation has spread all the way to Bolepur!' Tapasi said.

MAUNI BABA MET people everyday between four to five in the evening. The crowds he attracted were growing steadily as was his fame. Some magazines had already published articles on him. Tapasi and Uddhav reached Baba's place with Malay and Bholanath. They found a large number of people already waiting there, some silently pondering their own problems and worries, some conversing with others, a few of them unwell and moaning as they lay on the sheets they had spread on the sandstone platform.

Malay stood leaning against a wall. Tapasi sat quietly on the steps of the temple. She was asking Bholanath a lot of questions. About Kanika Di and Jatin Da's illness, the house, the garden, Vishwa Bharti, Didi's tea-stall. She wanted to know everything about them. But when Bholanath began telling her about Rakhal she told him to stop. Scattered clouds do not join together. They only change their shape. All she said was, 'Let it go, Kaka. There is no point re-opening old wounds. I don't want to know anything more.'

Tapasi moved away from Bholanath and glanced at Malay who stood at a distance. She noticed how serene and handsome he looked. A tall and impressive personality, with an attractive face. How could Lillian leave him, and why did she do it? She had a lot of questions in her mind but Malay's eyes seemed to have many more. The biggest question related to the deaths of Jatin Da and Kanika Di and the strange happenings since. The whole episode was puzzling. They were such decent, respectable people. You never heard any uncomplimentary thing about them. So how come their lives came to such an undesirable end? Tapasi knew that death was a vanquishing of all plans and expectations. So what unfinished business was not allowing Kanika Di's soul the peace of death? Tapasi wanted to hold Malay in her arms and lift him so high that no anxieties could ever reach and touch him. She longed to touch him and absorb all his worries into herself.

Bholanath had fallen into conversation with a Bengali gentleman who had come to meet Mauni Baba after visiting Mathura, bathing in the Yamuna and having darshan in the temples. The gentleman closed his eyes and recited a verse to Bholanath.

Yamune eiki tumisei yamune pravahini.
O jaar taley ruper haat vikant nilkant mani.

Tapasi thought it was a most beautiful description of the

Yamuna. 'O Yamuna, are you the one on whose banks existed the bazaar of Beauty where sapphires were sold?'

Ghanshyam, who was listening in to the conversation said, 'Yes, Tapasi Didi, the banks of Yamuna still have Beauty's bazaar and blue gemstones are still on sale there. The only thing lacking is the buyers.'

'What is the price of the blue gemstones, Ghanshyam?' Tapasi asked.

'A total surrender,' Ghanshyam answered.

'What a strange conversation!' Malay chipped in. 'What blue gemstones are you talking about?'

'I thought he meant sapphires as in precious stones,' Tapasi tried to explain.

'No, Tapasi Didi. It is not about sapphires. It is about the glimpses of the Lord, our Krishna Kanhaiya, who else?'

They fell silent but the gentleman near whom Bholanath was sitting was seen taking out a silver box from his pocket. He would put a pinch of something from the box in his mouth, close it and put it back in his pocket. Bholanath asked, 'Is that tobacco you are taking? Could I have some, please? In my hurry 1 forgot to carry my own.'

'It is not tobacco, my good fellow.'

'Is it paan masala then?'

'Not paan masala either. Before you ask your next question let me tell you, it is sand from the banks of the Yamuna.'

'What? Have you been eating sand all this while?' Everyone was astonished.

'How come you are eating the sand of this place though you are a Mussalman!' Ghanshyam asked.

'Yes, I am a Mussalman, and yet this sand is priceless to me. Someone told me an anecdote, which I'll relate to you. A friend of mine often went for walks near a graveyard where he always saw a couple of people talking cheerfully together. He thought they were gravediggers. One day he saw them weeping near a freshly dug grave. He asked, "What happened? Why are you crying? Have you lost a close relative?"

"Oh no," they answered. "We are spirits. The one who is buried here was to join our fraternity after death but he was gored and killed by a bull whose horns were powdered with the dust of Goverdhan Parvat. That dust reached the stomach of the deceased. So he did not become a ghost and gained a direct entry to Paradise."'

'O Ma!' Bholanath and Tapasi were astonished.

'Since then, my friend and I always carry small containers with this sacred dust with us.'

Bholanath, who was deeply affected by the story, had tears in his eyes. He turned to Malay and said, 'We seem to have come to the right place. My master and Didi Ma will sure find their deliverance here.' He lowered his voice and said further 'See, a Mussalman at this place?'

The stranger overheard him nevertheless. 'Yes, brother,' he said. 'A lot of people among us revere Lord Krishna. Do you know that there is a place called *Paakrooh Khatoon Ki Chhatri*. It is ancient and also recognized as Taj Ki Chhatri. Apparently, a lady named Taj Bibi was passing through Mathura on her pilgrimage to Kaaba Sharif. She was informed that Mathura was a sacred place where a God named Krishna resided. The lady cut short her journey and got off her vehicle in Mathura. She was restless and she called out,

'Suno diljani, merey dil ki kahani tum
Husn ki bikani, badnaami bhi sahoongi mein
Dev puja ki thaani, mein nimaz hoon bhulani
Tajey kalma quran, terey gunan kahoongi mein.'

(Listen my beloved, to the tale of my heart. I am a worshipper of your beauty who would gladly put up with notoriety for the sake of my love for you. Determined to worship you, I have abandoned Kalma and Quran. All I want now is to sing your praise).

Just then Mauni Baba's window opened. His disciple took the Muslim gentleman with him. Malay sat quietly holding Bholanath's hand as the latter addressed Tapasi. 'There is a legend, even about the dust of this place, Taposhi. What an amazing place!'

'Every experience here is different from the other. So much which is not normal has happened since I came back to India, Taposhi. 1 have a new experience every day. I am surprised that I know so little about my country, never knew it or maybe never had a chance to know it. Each wall, each rock, everything about it is so intriguing. The legends and myths associated with each thing are mindboggling. When I think of Ma, her rituals of worship, the way she talked—everything comes back to my mind with great intensity. Something from my inventory of sins seems to be tormenting her. I wonder what it is. Which of my mistakes could it be?' The Vilayati Babu Malay talked on as Tapasi, the rustic who was called uncouth once, listened attentively. Her mind was busy absorbing the depth of Malay's words and the essential meaning of the different kinds of experiences he had been undergoing.

Mauni Baba's disciple came upto them. 'Come, Tapasi. Baba is calling you.'

'Let us go, Malay, Bholanath Kaka.' Tapasi led them to Baba. Mauni Baba listened to Bholanath as he related his own version of the unusual happenings. Tapasi watched from a distance. Baba wrote a few words with white chalk on his slate. Malay copied them on a slip of paper after which Baba's window snapped shut.

Tapasi read the words on the slip of paper: 'Their souls are adrift because betrayal is a sin worse than murder. Man, not God, is responsible for his acts.'

◆◆◆

On the day of the shraaddh, a call came from Jaimala Devi. Ghanshyam took Tapasi to the telephone booth to talk to her. She said, 'Tapasi, your result has come and you have qualified with very good grades. You have to leave in fifteen days. You have to rush to Delhi. We have to get your passport, visa and air tickets.'

'Thank you, Jaya Didi.' There was a lump in her throat, 'I'll call you back. You've done so much for me.'

'Don't worry about anything. Just come over to Delhi.'

Ghanshyam was thrilled. He said excitedly, 'You have excelled yourself, Didi! You have reached the skies! It is really creditable the way you have risen above your circumstances to achieve such distinction. It is wonderful news. How come you look so sad?'

'I am thinking, Ghanshyam, as to why each dream of mine begins with a reference to death. Today is Jatin Da and Kanika Di's *shraadh*. They were an integral, invaluable part of my soul, my consciousness, my forbearance and my faith in life. Before them Teacher Didi...and...' She left the sentence unfinished.

◆◆◆

Uddhavji and Ghanshyam had arranged the materials for puja on Mauni Baba's platform. Dressed in a white dhoti and saffron *angavastra*, Malay sat looking like an ascetic in a forest. By now he had been convinced that such rituals were essential because their relevance was integral to every Indian's consciousness. Mauni Baba sat on his *aasan* with his eyes closed. Five priests sat close by reciting mantras. Nandita had joined Uddhav, Ghanshyam and Tapasi, who was deep in thought wondering if there was something beyond the enormous vacuum of death.

Kanika Di's ashes were placed in a small bronze vessel in front of the priests. A sacred ambience had been created by the loud chanting of mantras, the oblations of ghee to the holy fire and the rising aromatic smoke. According to the instructions of the presiding priest, flowers and grains of rice were being added to the ashes in the bronze vessel. Tapasi got up abruptly and left. It had become too much to bear.

THEIR LUGGAGE HAD been packed. Malay and Bholanath were going to Delhi in the same taxi as Tapasi. After taking leave of everybody, Tapasi got into the taxi and sat beside Malay in the passenger seat. Bholanath occupied the front seat. The taxi started and began to cruise steadily. Tapasi looked out of the moving taxi. Her eyes traversed the grave of the dead butterfly, the compound of the temple, the fixed stony eyes of Uddhavji's idol, Mauni Baba's room, the snake charmers' children, and the Kusum Sarovar before everything receded into the background.

Breaking the wistful silence, Malay said gently, 'Come

with me to Bolepur, Taposhi. Let me do something for you—something that might heal your wounds.'

'Thanks, but no, Malay. You have no role to play in my life. I don't want an obligation from you, please.'

'Really, Taposhi, you fascinate me. I never noticed you before, barely knew you. Otherwise you would not have been through so much suffering. Nandita has given me some idea of the hell you've been through. Anyway, Taposhi, come to Bolepur and pursue your dream. You could not study at Vishwa Bharti but you can teach there. I promise you a good life.'

Tapasi could not believe her ears. She had never heard such words in her life. How she had longed for what he was promising! After a moment's thought she said, 'Malay you don't know anything about my background or the history of my birth. Bholanath Kaka can tell you all. I don't know if my mother who sold her body in Sonagachhi is dead or alive. Maybe she too is a ghost, haunting some ancient ruin somewhere. I don't see why you should have any sympathy for me. I was cut out for this destiny. No one marries widows, Malay.'

'I don't care about other's opinions. You need not worry about them.'

'No, Malay. You don't know me. I'm like a valley where no flowers grow—where stones are tossed. I've never had the luxury of giving in to the demands of my body.'

Bholanath, who had been listening quietly to their conversation, pleaded from the front seat, 'Please come with us, Taposhi. Help us atone for Didi Ma and Maalik's betrayal.'

Tapasi interrupted him firmly, 'No, Kaka, no. Don't say a word. A play is at its most effective stage when the curtain falls at the end.'

The taxi came to a halt near a busy crossing in Delhi. Tapasi clearly understood her position. By now, she was fully convinced that this world, this heartless world of reality, was never going to open a door of happiness for her. Precious words like 'dreams' and 'happiness' lose their meaning through repetition. At the present crossroads in her life she realized that she needed intervention from nobody and she did not want to be obliged to anyone. The past with its thorny torments was enough to convince her that she was completely alone in this world. Her reality was exclusive to her. She had to search for it by treading its path on her own feet, and to find it if she was destined to do so. Tapasi opened the car door and strode towards Jaimala Devi's house without a backward glance.

JAIMALA DEVI HAD arranged for Tapasi to stay in her brother's house in Delhi. Her time there was like a training programme for her. During this time, she had to prepare herself for America and her new life there. Her host's daughter, Vasundhara, had already initiated her in the ways of polite society and taught her to dress tastefully. She had mastered table etiquette and could eat with a knife and fork. But there were so many formalities to be completed before she could leave. The passport, the visa, the medical insurance. The insurance people said they needed her to have a battery of medical tests as she had lived in such unhygienic conditions. Vasundhara arranged for the family doctor to examine her and personally paid for all the tests and investigations he ordered. Tapasi was touched by the display of extra affection, compassion and intimacy. The family had no prejudices. They treated Tapasi as an equal who was being groomed by them. The long forgotten phrase, 'polite laughter', often came to her mind. Living with them in their house she often remembered Jatin Da and Kanika Di. They too had contributed to the development of her personality. In those days, she had never imagined that her destiny would take her so far. She often looked with disbelief at the file containing her result sheets for the exams she had taken as well as the letter from Cornell University confirming her admission to the course of higher study there.

Vasundhara's health had taken a turn for the worse and she kept falling ill frequently. She even spent a few days in the hospital every now and then. Poor health must have been the reason she had not married though she was over thirty-five years of age. Tapasi did not ask questions relating to personal matters nor did she exercise her freedom to ask the reasons behind certain things. However, she was observant enough to see how concerned Jaimala Devi and her brother were about Vasundhara's health.

Living in a congenial atmosphere, she was nursing hopes and aspirations of going to a far-off place where her dream of academic achievement would come true. She was looking forward to a life in an unfamiliar place where she would transcend both her tormented past and her austere but relatively dignified existence in Goverdhan till recently. During her stay in Delhi, all her dreams, her trust and her entire consciousness were centered on that house. It is another matter that countless questions relating to her past still troubled her mind and at times she had misgivings about her future. She often tried to visualize Cornell University which had enrolled her after she had cleared just a few question papers—a place which had accepted her with all her deficiencies. She was aware of how much Jaimala Devi was spending to give her a meaningful future. Tapasi's ardent desire and academic aspirations had led her to a stage where Vasundhara was giving her greater moral support than even Jaimala Devi. They were going all out to wipe off the stigma of poverty and widowhood that had clung to her. The time of her departure was drawing close. Through the efforts of Jaimala Devi and Vasundhara, the passport, visa, health insurance papers and other documents had been obtained and Tapasi was looking forward to a great future. She was gradually slipping out of the mould of one held ransom by tradition and social convention. She was riding on the currents of a great dream.

◆◆◆

Entering the unfamiliar ambience of the aircraft, Tapasi was nervous but she tried her best to remain calm. She occupied the seat that the air hostess showed her. She went over all the warnings and precautions mentioned by Vasundhara, and wrapped a protective silence around her like a shawl. Accompanied by a short welcome on the public address system, the aircraft took off, circled the airport and rose higher and higher, leaving the ground far away. She felt as if the clouds had buoyed up the plane whose shadow falling on the clouds at a lower level made it look like a large bird flying with its wings spread out. She wondered if Kanika Di's soul resided in those clouds. After all those pujas and oblations, had Kanika Di and Jatin Da's souls found deliverance, or were they still haunting the house where fragrances had colours? She herself had found deliverance after eight years of suffering. Her lot had not been in any way less tormented than that of the disembodied spirits whose funeral rites had not been completed. Anyway, her latest journey was not just a physical one, it was simultaneously a journey of the soul which had delivered her from her initial setbacks and restored her to her old self. She had come to the sacred region of Braj from Bengal. She had traversed that ground barefoot along with several compatriots—compatriots she had left behind at each milestone. Ambika Devi, Barota, Mariam, Vrinda, the exalted truth of the tongueless journalist on the door of death, Mauni Baba and then Jaimala Devi and Vasundhara. They had all played significant roles in her life. Extraordinary characters—all of them.

She took out her old blue notebook from her small handbag, opened it and placed it on her knees. Its pages had turned yellow and musty. There were pages with old names, anecdotes and reminiscences written in a childish hand. She turned the pages and came to one on which she had noted down the address of Jaimala Devi's younger brother. The letter of fellowship from her college was also kept in the blue notebook. That address and the letter were her bridge to New York. Jaimala Devi's brother was to receive her at the airport. Some people emerge from nowhere to lend a helping hand to others. But suppose he did not turn up? A question again. Tapasi told herself that she should not have such misgivings. Jaimala Devi had talked to him over the phone. He was bound to come to the airport. Tapasi was Prashna once again. Why were there always questions in her mind? Questions had been with her at every stage of her life. They were the sole testimony to her existence. She had flowed along the currents of Time on the strength of her questions. Like the limitless sky stretched outside, they were the only space of her creation and so they would remain.

She closed her eyes. A kind of music came floating on the breeze—a cosmic rhythm rising towards her after circumambulating sacred places. She seemed to be turned into *anhad naad*, which was gently soothing away all the undeserved suffering she had undergone.

Suddenly, she looked out of the window and noticed that there was absolutely nothing outside—no clouds, sun, moon or stars. What she was looking at was utterly different from a tangible universe—it was just empty space all around. In that dream-like state, Tapasi was suddenly convinced that the wandering spirits of the dead must definitely be finding peace in that enormous, accepting empty space.

She closed her eyes again with a sleep induced by the reassuring knowledge that all was well.

WAKING FROM A deep sleep, Tapasi wondered why the view was so different when she opened her eyes. Why was the air around her so heavy and so full of unpleasant smells? What had happened to the soft piped music and the pleasantly perfumed air-conditioning of the aircraft? In an instant she become conscious that she was not sitting on the cushioned seat of an aeroplane. She was lying on her back on a hard iron bed and her body was covered with a grimy white sheet. She patted her body to figure out what had happened. Had her plane crashed? Black misgivings, a deep despair, disillusionment and horror filled her.

'Where am I? Will someone tell me where I am?' she screamed. Why does any forward movement always push me back? Why have I suffered only setbacks all my life?

Her screams penetrated the heavy air once again.

'Oh, she has regained consciousness,' she heard someone say disinterestedly from a corner of the room. Tapasi tried to get up but her body felt like a rock. Her head throbbed when she moved it.

'What happened to me? Why doesn't anybody tell me anything?'

A nurse came over and stood by the bed. 'What do you want to know? Ask me and I'll tell you,' she said shortly.

Tapasi tried to establish a rapport with her but the nurse had an expressionless face and she spoke sternly. 'Don't move so much. Look, this needle has been displaced and so much blood has spilled.'

'Please tell me where I am.'

'You are in Delhi. In a hospital.'

'What happened to me? How did I get here?'

'You were found lying unconscious on the road. You were admitted here by a good Samaritan. Your appendix ruptured. Do you know what an appendix is? Never mind. You had to undergo surgery to remove it. Okay, lie still now. I will give you an injection.' The nurse administered an injection. Tapasi felt her body with her free hand and discovered that her abdomen was covered with a huge bandage. Intense pain shook her down to her soul, like a yellow leaf in a storm—a leaf which never turned green—a frail, trembling leaf barely touched by the sunshine of hope.

'Oh, this pain—I don't know what the hell this pain is, it's driving me...!'

The injection had taken effect. She passed out.

Every time Tapasi came to, she would groan and scream. She would call out to Jaimala Devi and Vasundhara. Each time, she was injected and packed off into oblivion again. Drifting between sleep and wakefulness, one moment she would feel that she was flying towards the realization of her dreams but the very next she would be reminded of the turn of events which had landed her, shattered and injured, into the crumpled, dirty sheets of a hospital bed.

◆◆◆

She gazed outside the window. It was raining but the drizzle was so faint it seemed as if the clouds were weeping silent tears. In spite of the drizzle there were layers of dust on the branches of a tree that she could see through the window. Hospital sounds of pain and suffering combined with the dust-laden tree in the faint drizzle to create an ambience of pathetic regret. No clouds were visible from the window. The view was blocked by the yellowish wall of an adjacent building that hung in the air like hollow, mirthless laughter. Tapasi turned her eyes away. She felt a stab of acute, unbearable pain and put her hand under the covers to feel the large bandage on her abdomen. The pain seemed to be rising from its hiding place, where it lurked, coiled up under layers of medicine, dressing and stitches. Now it had snaked through the protective layers to come out and sit threateningly upon her chest. Helplessly, she began to groan but there was no one to soothe her pain. There was no one in the room to listen to her cries. All the beds in the room, except one, were unoccupied. A woman lay unmoving, in deep comatose sleep, on a bed in the far corner of the room. There were no doctors or nurses anywhere.

A woman attendant came at fixed times to the room. She brought spartan meals of khitchri, rice and tea twice a day. The nurse on duty came once a day to check her pulse and hand her a tablet. She would also give her an injection under whose influence Tapasi would fall into a stuperous, hallucinogenic sleep, a dark hole from which her paralysed mind fought to escape. She lost all sense of time. It seemed to seep out of her body through the needle in her arm. Slowly a dark cloud descended upon her eyes and she drifted into an uneasy, drug-induced sleep.

By now, Tapasi had understood the connection between the injections and the state of oblivion. One fine day she resolved to fight off the sleep for she had noticed the circular incision on her abdomen during a change of dressing. As the doctor cleaned and dressed it, she had discovered that the wound had not healed in any significant way. She could hear voices talking as she lay with her eyes closed, pretending sleep.

Through half-closed eyes Tapasi could see the white uniform of the nurse and a rustling, almond-coloured silk sari. She also heard a whispered conversation.

'So, Doctor, the girl is all right now, is she not? Has the wound healed nicely? When will you discharge her?'

The soft voice sounded familiar, gentle, cadenced, riding aloft an aromatic cloud of incense that now merged, now mingled with the antiseptic smells of the hospital.

'Yes, she is okay. The wound is healing. As Bhaiji instructed us, we are keeping her sedated because once she is fully conscious and finds out that one of her kidneys has been removed, she might go into shock.'

'Has Vasundhara's body accepted her kidney properly, Doctor?'

'Yes, the implant has been successful. Don't worry. She'll soon be absolutely normal. She'll be perfectly healthy in a few days.'

'And how about this girl... Tapasi?' The soft voice asked.

'She'll take time. Donors normally regret their decision. Very often they go into depression.'

'But, Doctor, she has been told that she had an appendectomy. She knows nothing about the kidney.'

Tapasi, who was half-conscious now, began to feel the pain like a punch in her stomach. Before she could lose consciousness, she grabbed the doctor's arm and screamed with all her might, 'Oh, Doctor—it hurts!' Her half-closed eyes could barely comprehend the horrible truth. She saw Jaimala Devi and Vasundhara's father. Their faces as impassive and clinically-detached as the doctor's.

'You'll be all right. Absolutely normal,' the doctor said.

'She will be normal...Vasundhara will be, Doctor. But how about me?'

She tried to sit up and snapped some of the sutures in the wound. Blood began to ooze out of the incision. The nurse held her by the shoulders and forced her to lie down again.

'Give her an injection at once, nurse. Didn't you give

her one in the morning? Looks like she has heard everything due to your negligence. She can become delirious. Her temperature is rising.'

The nurse began to prepare an injection. Tapasi gazed at Jaimala Devi with tears rolling down her cheeks. The doctor administered the injection. Before she drifted into oblivion, she heard him say, 'Call someone from her family to be with her. She lies alone all the time. How long can we keep her drugged? There should be someone to provide moral support to her. Emotional support is absolutely essential after major surgery like hers. You must have paid her a huge sum as compensation.'

The medicines began to have their effect. An arbitrary darkness surrounded her and the bottomless vastness of Hades opened its jaws to swallow her up.

SOMEONE WAS HOLDING her hand and calling out her name. 'Tapasi, Tapasi.'

Nandita?

Tapasi blinked her eyes. Yes, it was her. She blinked again. Did that mean she was dreaming once more? From the tranquil music of the aircraft to the deep silence of a hospital. And now Nandita. How come she is here? Tapasi wondered. Her mind cleared a bit, and her thought processes re-emerged, like vapour from a pot of boiling water.

Nandita was sitting on a stool by her bedside. It was true. She stretched out her free hand and touched Nandita with fingers trembling in disbelief. Her voice, emerging from the cover of sleep, was tremulous. 'Nandita? Here? Please, Nandita, tell me the truth. How did I get into this mess? No one tells me anything.'

'Yes, Tapasi, I am here and I have come to see you after Ghanshyam informed me about you. Tapasi, you are in a hospital in Delhi. You have been operated on. One of your kidneys has been surgically removed and implanted into Jaimalaji's niece, Vasundhara. She was dangerously ill and they could not find a donor so you have been made the sacrificial beast.''

The tree outside the window had been uprooted by the rain and storm of the previous night. The gardeners and orderlies of the hospital were busy hacking its branches. From somewhere in the distance came the sound of an old ramshackle bus rattling by.

Nandita helped Tapasi to sit up and placed a pillow behind her back. Tapasi held Nandita with a feeble hand trembling in pain.

'God knows after how many days I have sat up,' she said, 'My back is stiff as a plank.'

'You've been in hospital for about two weeks. Come, let me rub your back.' Nandita began to massage her back but stopped short, 'Oh, what a big bandage!'

'I don't know when they'll take it off. When will I be able to stand on my feet?'

'Soon,' Nandita said reassuringly.

'Nandita, can one survive on one kidney? Do you think I'll have normal health again?'

'I'll change your clothes.' Nandita tried to evade giving an answer. From under the bed, she pulled out the handbag that Tapasi had packed for her journey abroad. Then she said, 'Yes, Tapasi. It is possible to live with one kidney. The doctor was saying that some people are born with only one kidney and they live a full, normal, healthy life. As for you, you have given Vasundhara a new lease of life with your kidney. Her good wishes are with you.'

'Nandita, I am so bewildered. Jaimalaji and her family treated me with so much love that I put all my sorrows behind me and began to look forward to a great future, but then they reduced me to this... If only they had asked, let alone a kidney, I'd happily have given my life for them. But to deceive and betray me like this? What a cruel joke!'

'You are right, Tapasi. I'm also surprised at their duplicity. But to tell you the truth, I often had some misgiving, about why she was so effusive with her affections for you. She went all out to support you in every way.' Nandita reflected for a moment and then asked abruptly, 'How about your passport?'

'It must be in that bag. My file must also be in it. Look carefully for "Cornell University" written on it.'

Nandita turned the bag upside down but except for a few clothes, the only other things in the bag were her old blue notebook and some money in a small wallet.

'What is all this? What does it mean?' Tapasi tried to probe her benumbed mind for an answer but came up with nothing more than a deepening incomprehension.

'Was your passport made at all or was that a pretence as well?'

'As far as I can remember, the passport was made. Maybe they've kept it with them. But where shall I go from here? What should I do?'

'Do you know, Tapasi, that you are in the general ward and Vasundhara is recuperating in the expensive private ward? I am not sure that you are even receiving proper medical care. As far as I can understand, they are keeping you drugged but tranquillizers are not the treatment for a surgical wound.'

'I can't believe that Jaimalaji would treat me this way, Nandita, I had unshakeable faith in her—the same faith I had in Kanika Di and Jiten Da. I trusted her with my future, my life. What will happen to all my hard work now, Nandita?'

'Come back to Goverdhan. Come and live where you were. With such frail health you have no alternative.'

'I'm not sure I'll be able to live there anymore. Every inch of that place is witness to my boundless love and trust in Jaimalaji. How can I live there with all that love and faith shattered and betrayed?'

A nurse materialized suddenly and admonished Nandita. 'You'd better leave now. Visiting hour is over.'

My time was over a long time ago, thought Tapasi to herself. She looked at the nurse. The contemptuous way she spoke, her bored, listless expression, her tight smile, her white uniform heavy with the smell of antibiotics and her thermometer dipped in a yellow substance—all bespoke a sick mentality. Nandita examined the medicines on the tray and said to the nurse, 'Sister, you have not given her any antibiotics. How will her wound heal?'

'What can we do? We have to follow the doctor's instructions. Okay now, you better leave. The time is up.'

'I'll come again, Tapasi,' Nandita said and moved away reluctantly.

Nandita left. It seemed to Tapasi that everybody—known, unknown, familiar or unfamiliar—was out of the purview of her circle of hope. She expected nothing from anyone. There was a definite dividing line between the reality of Jaimala Devi, Bhaiji and Vasundhara on the one hand and her illusionary world of exam results, the invitation to Cornell University, and a passport with a wistful-faced young woman's photograph on it. Where was Jaimala Devi's idealism and her soft, compassionate voice? She had played with Tapasi, wearing a mask of compassion as she'd cold-bloodedly rolled the dice, staking not only Tapasi's future but whatever miserable life she was left with. Was there any difference between Ambika Devi and her? Had she been sold to Jaimala Devi? Had she been promised the chance to lead a fulfilling, useful life only as a ruse to get her kidney?

Tapasi figured out that the entire manipulation had been conducted with Ambika Devi's connivance. Teaching in the school and living under Jaimala Devi's care had only been a pretext. Her mind went back to all the blood tests and visits to the doctor that Jaimala Devi had so solicitously lined up for the schoolchildren and the teachers. Had it all been a screening test for the right donor? Tapasi was a product sold to a trading company—just an ordinary body. It was another matter, and an inconsequential one, that inside that body was a sensitive heart and a brilliant mind.

Her sense of misery and destitution was worsened by her blighted faith, a broken body and a heart emptied of all desire. What needed to be seen now was whether Nandita was also playing a major part in the whole play.

◆◆◆

'Come, Tapasi, come with me. I'll take you to a good doctor who'll treat you properly. You can stay with me. Once you are feeling better, we'll think about what you can do in the future.'

'Future? Whose future are you talking about?' Tapasi had to measure herself on her own scales. Leaning on Nandita's arm, she stepped out of the prison house of the hospital. The time of reckoning had slipped away again. When she was about to leave for America her heart had been aglow with anticipation, she'd worn new shoes on her feet, but now her heart was cold with dejection and her feet unsteady with weakness. Why is change so unrelenting? Why are the streets so narrow that you can't see much ahead of you? Why is my fate so sadistically perverse? Prashna Tapasi was being jolted alive by the bumpy auto rickshaw in which Nandita was taking her home.

The doctor that Nandita took her to changed her dressing and wrote out a prescription. He spoke to Nandita, 'Look, she needs a lot of care and looking after. Her wound is still raw. Without proper care it can go septic. She should be given all her medicines regularly as well as a nutritious diet.'

'My wounds have always been raw, but like a fool I thought that they had healed and in those heady, delusional days, I began to feel that I too had a right to dream. I don't know how I forgot that I was only a tiny lump of clay on the giant potter's wheel. My feet have been created to lead me to the cremation ground, not to an aircraft,' Tapasi said to Nandita.

'Don't lose heart, Tapasi,' Nandita replied soothingly. 'Get well first, then we'll see what we can do.'

The obvious fate of an uprooted tree is that it crashes to the ground. But Nandita was still steering her towards hope. Is it possible for dry leaves to turn green again?

◆◆◆

Staying with Nandita and under her solicitous care, Tapasi's condition improved to some degree. She began to feel stronger but was perturbed by the whispered arguments between Nandita and Ranbir over her. Tapasi resolved to remove herself from Nandita's house before Ranbir's resentment of her flared up into a domestic crisis. She was deeply disturbed by the unfriendly expression on Ranbir's face and the abnormal distance the children maintained from her. As for Nandita, she was caught between the contrary pulls of her concern for Tapasi and her devotion to her husband.

'I am fine now, Nandita. I'm strong enough to travel. Please do me one more favour. Put me on a train to Kolkata. I've been longing to go to Bolepur.'

She had packed her belongings into her handbag.

THERE WOULD BE no mysteries in life if one understood every new situation that presented itself. All the hopes and illusions in one's mind would crumble, reduced to ash, like the colourful wings of a dead butterfly. Ever since the knowledge of her circumstances had dawned upon her, all the questions in Tapasi's mind had been dying a slow death. Her questions, the intense desire for knowledge, had once been the driving force of her life. She had lived for them. They made her think about life and gave connection and continuity to her eagerness for knowledge, for love and for relationships. It was her questioning mind that had guided her path like a beacon of light through all kinds of situations. But this time over she had admitted defeat. Perhaps because the wound in her body had not healed. In fact, it had grown worse.

She boarded the second class compartment with unsteady steps, carrying her small bag in her hand. Nandita had packed rotis and subzi in a plastic box for her to eat on the train. She had also given her a bottle of water. Tapasi swallowed some painkillers and settled down in her seat. The compartment was crowded but she had no desire to strike up a conversation with anyone. As it was, the rickshaw ride from the town to the railway station had exhausted her and aggravated the pain.

The train rattled to a start and then slowly picked up speed. Someone was asking for her ticket. She fumbled through her bag and found a white envelope containing the ticket and a few currency notes. The ticket collector left. Tapasi counted the money. There were ten one hundred rupee notes in all. Tapasi was filled with gratitude for Nandita. But immediately her gratitude gave way to painful scepticism. After all, she thought, a necklace can't be strung without a string. Without a string how would the pearls hold together? Had Nandita been in on the conspiracy against her all along?

The train went through a long tunnel—hollow, empty dark and endless. Tapasi was falling into a deeper and deeper gloom. Dusk began to fall. The sky was no longer blue. It was growing darker by degrees. A few clouds wandered here and there, seeming to mull over the discarded dreams Tapasi had banished from her mind. Perhaps, that was the reason why she felt a deep peace within herself. The peace was akin to the profound calm that prevails after the din of a battle, when all dissent is silenced by decisive and lethal action.

'Will you have something? A cold drink? Orange?' A man in a khaki uniform stood in front of her holding a bucket full of cold drink bottles.

'Yes, I will. Please give me an orange.'

She was very thirsty. The other passengers were eating and drinking too. Some were already asleep. Others were lost in themselves or peering outside the windows. Tapasi felt better after drinking the soft drink.

'Where are you going?' The middle-aged man with a bespectacled, nondescript face sitting next to her asked.

'Kolkata,' Tapasi answered briefly. And you?' she asked for the sake of etiquette.

'I am going to Dhanbad.'

'What do you do there?'

'I am an accountant in a government office. I am going there on business.'

'I see.' Tapasi wished to remain silent. Her questions were all finished—questions, which had once so crowded her mind.

'Do you belong to Kolkata?' The man asked again.

'No, I am from a small town near Kolkata.' She deliberately did not mention Bolepur because the very mention of that place made her think of Vishwa Bharti and Tagore and that would wreck her calm. She looked out of the window. Though she'd taken her pills some time ago, the sharp twinges of pain in her wound refused to subside.

'Are you unwell?' The man asked.

'Yes. I had an operation.'

'Oh!' He shifted to make a little more space for Tapasi to sit comfortably, then opened his newspaper and began to read. Tapasi wanted to sleep but couldn't so she borrowed a page of the newspaper. Her eyes fell on a small advertisement:

'Wanted—a donor with healthy kidneys. The donor will be paid a reward of one lakh rupees and full expenses for treatment and hospitalization will be borne by the advertiser.'

She sat still for a long moment with the sheet of newspaper lying in her lap. It was getting dark now. She wondered what her journey signified. Ten one hundred rupee notes in an envelope, the bandage on her stomach, spasms of pain inside her. Was this haphazard escape from her recent circumstances a break from all her suffering till date, the ultimate frontier of pain, or a last ditch attempt to protect her from killing herself? Let it be whatever it was. She was not going to think about it any more.

The train was approaching a station. It slowed down but did not halt. Soon the station receded like an island of lights in the background. She had left a whole lot of things behind: her metamorphosis into a cultured, graceful woman, her feeling of self esteem, her aspiration for a genteel lifestyle—all these had evaporated and blended into a bloodied circle of unexpected events.

Tapasi sensed that the wound in her abdomen had opened again and that the pus stained blood was oozing from it drop by drop. But she was determined to reach Bolepur, to go to Rakhal Kaka perhaps, to that small house with the huge banyan tree in front. She had to reach the princes, the soldiers and the watchmen of her dreams, entwined in the aerial roots of the banyan tree. And to seek out the vague figure hiding behind the broken bullock cart who had left her the bangle on her wedding day, whom she did not know, or perhaps whom she did. And what of Malay who had held her hand and pleaded on the way to Delhi from Vrindavan, 'Let me do something for you, Tapasi. Come with me to Bolepur.'

The letter from Cornell had helped her overcome all the complexes in her subconscious mind. It was her triumph and her solace. That sheet of paper had been testimony to her personal achievement, an exclusive triumph of herself on the basis of which she had declined Malay's offer and walked abruptly away. That was the day, the only day in her life, when for a moment she had really been someone. That she had felt touched by the radiance of the sun. She had had new chappals on her feet, fine new clothes on her body. She had embarked on a journey through the skies with a dignity achieved by her own efforts. After that brief moment in which she had breathed freely as a human being what followed was total devastation, the annihilation of all her energies.

Tapasi could feel the inner layers of her dressing get soaked with blood. The passenger sitting next to her had got off at an earlier station. The unknown stranger and his anonymous face merged with the masks of her past. All those forgotten faces and their names floated inside and outside Tapasi in the gloom of the railway compartment.

They seemed to be scratching her, clawing her, biting her with their teeth, nibbling at her, reducing her to an utter wretchedness, which shook her confidence and strength all over again. Her world was rocking to and fro. Her mind, her thoughts, her very soul, were drowning within her.

The train approached Howrah station and immediately there was commotion and excitement in the compartment. All the passengers got up in a hurry. In the melee of luggage, baskets, bundles, women, children pushing and jostling with impatience, there was a huge sense of relief at having arrived at one's destination.

A coolie clad in a red kurta came and stood before Tapasi. 'Ma, O Ma, your luggage?'

Tapasi felt an unfamiliar warmth in his address, a oneness evoked by his distinctively Bolepur accent, a sense of belonging to the same place. Holding her suffering close to her self, she handed him her bag and began to get off the coach. Her feet were not comfortable in the new chappals. Her foot twisted and she fell forward. Something sharp jutting out of the railing or from a heavy steel trunk lying on the platform pierced the bandage on her abdomen. The coolie made a desperate effort to prevent the half-conscious Tapasi from falling but in vain. Blood and pus from her septic wound had already seeped through the folds of her sari. The coolie picked her up and laid her on a bench. The blood gushed out like a fountain. The coolie got extremely nervous. He placed her bag near her and beat a hasty retreat.

Though still semi-conscious, Tapasi was not really anxious or worried. She was familiar with pain. She covered the bloodstained parts of her body with the newspaper she had in her hand but the deep red drops of blood continued to seep through. When a sudden invigorating breeze blew in her direction, she breathed deeply, trying to revive herself. She did not know where the breeze had come from. A slight gust of wind is as capable of fanning the weak flame of an oil lamp, as it is of snuffing it out. Someone had picked the newspaper off her stomach and was fanning her with it. There it was again, that kidney donation advertisement. An old ramshackle fan whirred on the ceiling of the platform. A few pigeons fluttered about. Am I dreaming or is this real? Why does everything seem to be happening in a vacuum? Am I in my body or have I transcended it?

Her tired eyes rested on a sloka from the Bhagavad scribbled on a wall streaked with paan juice and soiled with grime—*Yatha arbhak swa pratibimba vibhramah:* (The egotism of mortals is the food of the Supreme Soul.) Did Krishna vanish abruptly in the middle of *raaslila* just to vanquish the ego of the gopis? Tapasi felt herself beginning to fade out. She could see a bridge of light beckoning her, she could feel her soul spiral into space.

◆◆◆

'Whose corpse is this? Any idea?'

'There's no identification.'

Tapasi's bloodsoaked body lay covered with a newspaper.

Questions change their course. Ideas and emotions change direction. Dead questions get crushed under the wheels of fearsome railway trains.

But some questions are eternal…